T0039862

INSTANT WALL ART:

VINTAGE MAP PRINTS

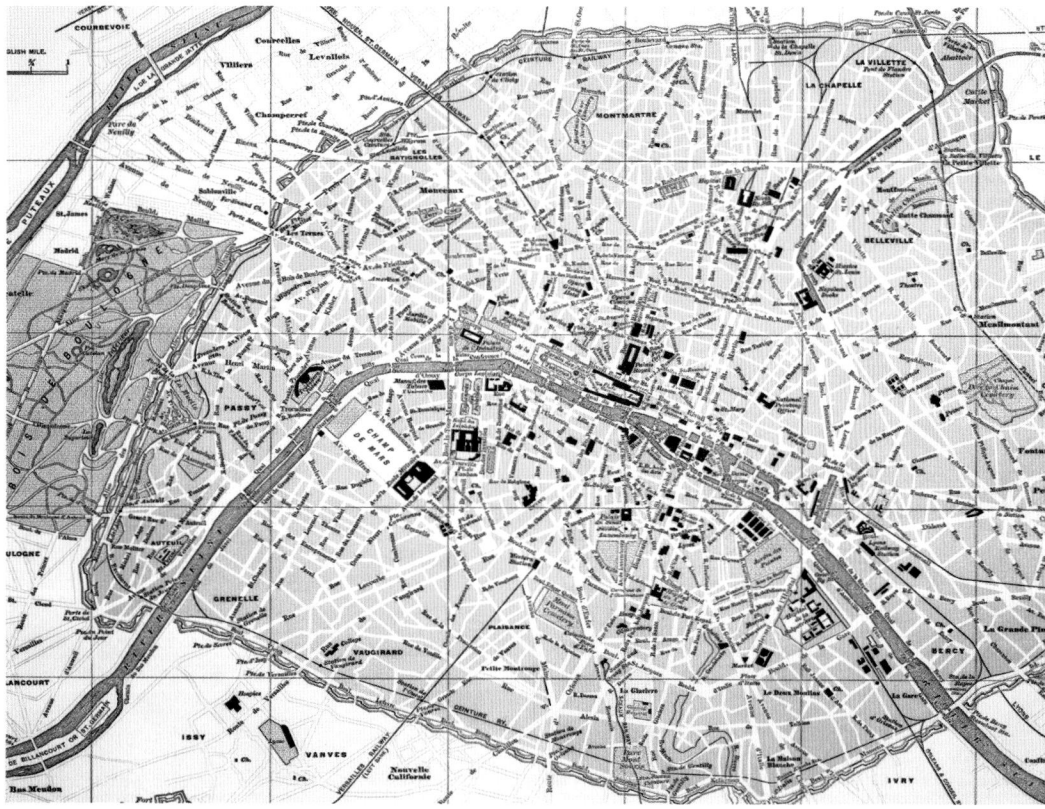

45 READY-TO-FRAME ILLUSTRATIONS FOR YOUR HOME DÉCOR

Adams Media
New York London Toronto Sydney New Delhi

adamsmedia
Adams Media
An Imprint of Simon & Schuster, Inc.
57 Littlefield Street
Avon, Massachusetts 02322

Copyright © 2017 by Simon & Schuster, Inc.

All rights reserved, including the right to reproduce this book or portions thereof in any form whatsoever. For information address Adams Media Subsidiary Rights Department, 1230 Avenue of the Americas, New York, NY 10020.

First Adams Media trade paperback edition DECEMBER 2017

ADAMS MEDIA and colophon are trademarks of Simon and Schuster.

For information about special discounts for bulk purchases, please contacta Simon & Schuster Special Sales at 1-866-506-1949 or business@simonandschuster.com.

The Simon & Schuster Speakers Bureau can bring authors to your live event. For more information or to book an event contact the Simon & Schuster Speakers Bureau at 1-866-248-3049 or visit our website at www.simonspeakers.com.

Interior design by Sylvia McArdle

Manufactured in the United States of America

10 9 8 7 6 5 4 3 2 1

ISBN 978-1-5072-0589-1

Many of the designations used by manufacturers and sellers to distinguish their products are claimed as trademarks. Where those designations appear in this book and Simon & Schuster, Inc., was aware of a trademark claim, the designations have been printed with initial capital letters.

INTRODUCTION

Today, beautifully colored vintage maps are showing up everywhere you look—from popular design magazines and websites to the walls of your friends' living rooms and kitchens. And now, instead of having to choose between one or two expensive prints, you can choose from the forty-five beautiful illustrations found within the pages of *Instant Wall Art: Vintage Map Prints* to personalize your own walls!

From maps of the stars to some of the world's biggest cities, these prints span a variety of locations and time periods with muted colors and fine details that capture the beauty of the land, sea, and sky. Now, with images ranging from the streets of New York City to the London Underground to a view of the North Pole, you're sure to find something in this book that speaks to your design aesthetic. These map prints measure 8" × 10" and will fit in a standard mat and frame once removed from the book at the perforated edge. So choose the prints you love, hang them on your walls, and enjoy their elegance in your own home year round!

THE PRINTS

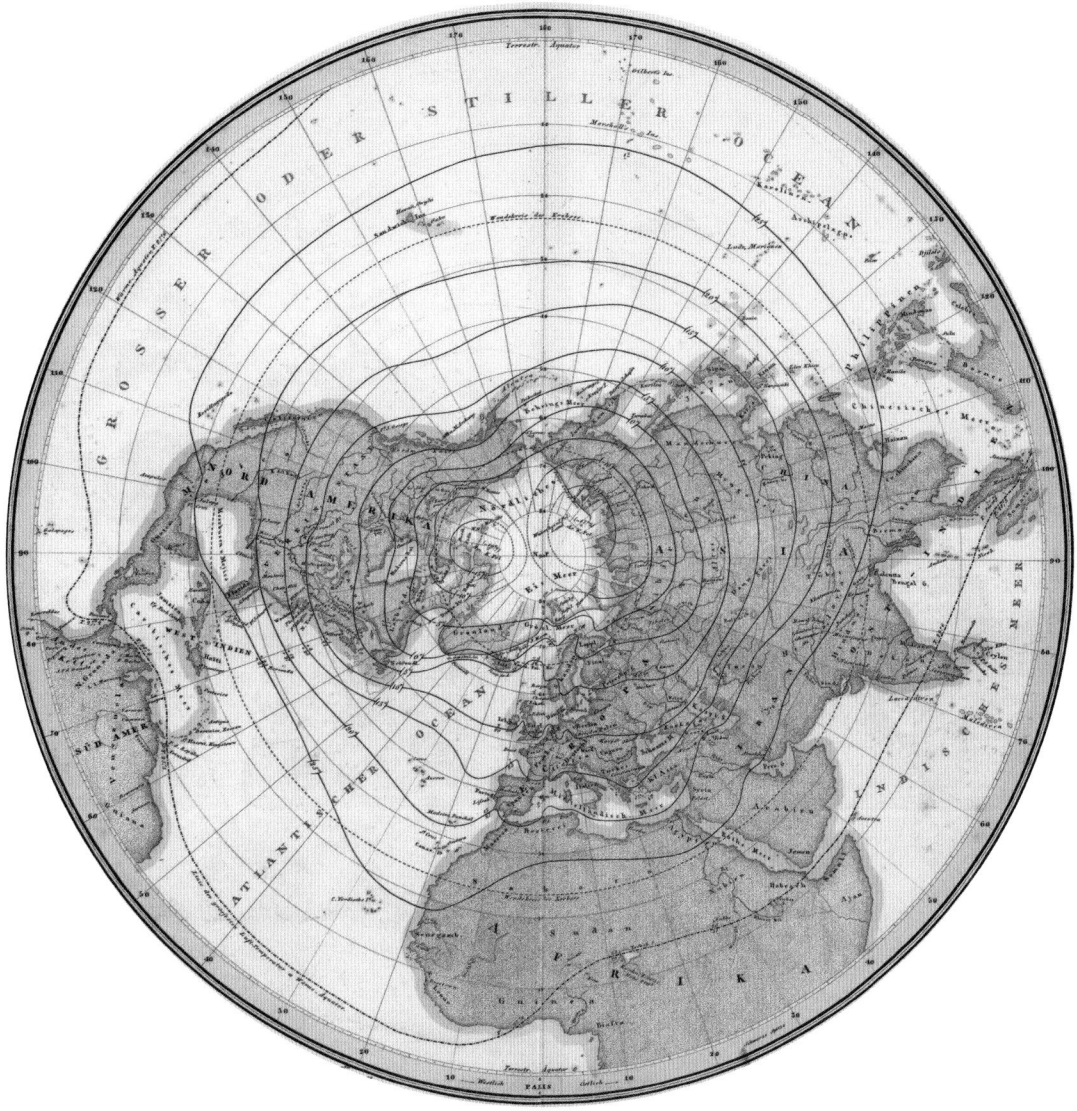
GROSSER OEST LICHER OCEAN
NORD AMERIKA
SÜD AMERIKA
ATLANTISCHER OCEAN
INDISCHER OCEAN
ASIA
AFRIKA
Arabien
Terrestr. Aequator

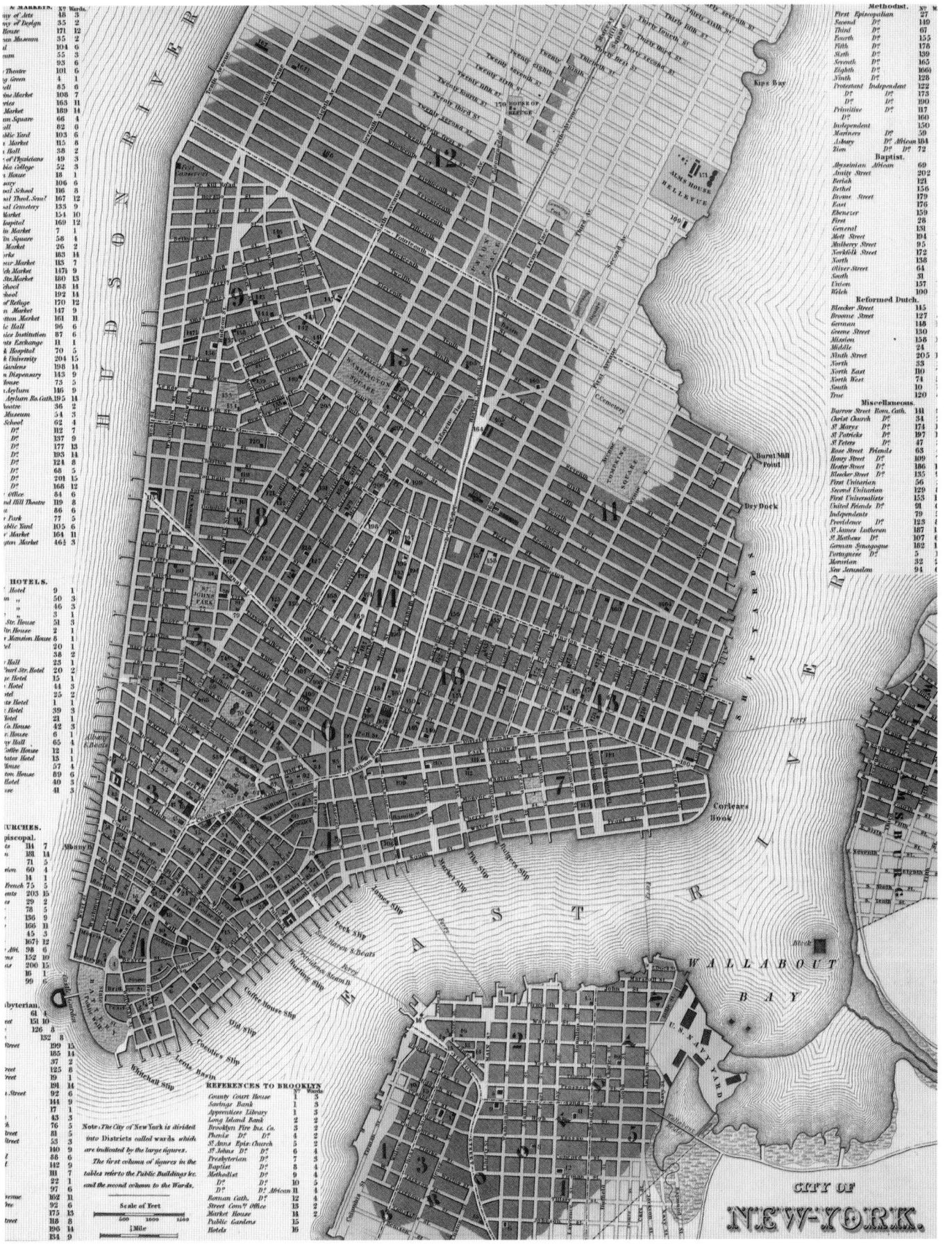

		Wards.
MARKETS.		
...y of Arts	48	3
...y of Design	35	2
...House	171	12
...an Museum	35	2
...l	104	6
...um	55	3
	93	6
...Theatre	101	6
...y Green	4	1
...ell	85	6
...ine Market	106	7
...ter	163	11
...Market	189	14
...an Square	66	4
...ell	82	6
...blic Yard	103	6
...Market	115	8
...Hall	38	2
...of Physicians	49	3
...bia College	52	3
...House	18	1
...sary	106	6
...ol School	116	8
...ol Theol. Sem.y	167	12
...al Cemetery	133	9
...Market	154	10
...hospital	169	12
...n Market	7	1
...n Square	58	4
...Market	26	2
...rks	163	14
...our Market	113	7
...ch Market	147½	9
...Ste. Market	180	13
...chool	183	14
...chool	192	14
...of Refuge	170	12
...n Market	147	9
...ton Market	161	11
...e Hall	96	6
...ice Institution	87	6
...nts Exchange	11	1
...k Hospital	70	5
...k University	204	15
...dens	193	14
...s Dispensary	143	9
...House	73	5
...Asylum	146	9
...Asylum Ro. Cath.	195	14
...heatre	36	2
...Museum	54	3
...School	62	4
...D.o	112	7
...D.o	137	9
...D.o	177	13
...D.o	193	14
...D.o	124	8
...D.o	68	5
...D.o	201	15
...D.o	168	12
...Office	84	6
...nd Hill Theatre	119	8
...e	86	6
...r Park	77	5
...ublic Yard	105	6
...r Market	164	11
...gton Market	46½	3
HOTELS.		
...Hotel	9	1
...n "	50	3
"	46	3
"	3	1
...Str. House	51	3
...Str. House	2	1
...r Mansion House	6	1
...el	20	1
	38	2
...Hall	23	1
...Court Str. Hotel	20	2
...ge Hotel	15	1
...Hotel	44	3
...tel	25	2
...ts Hotel	1	1
...Hotel	39	3
...Hotel	21	1
...Co. House	42	3
...e House	6	1
...ny Hall	65	4
...Coffee House	12	1
...ates Hotel	13	1
...House	57	4
...ton House	89	6
...Hotel	40	3
...use	41	3
CHURCHES.		
...piscopal.		
...ts	114	7
...n	193	14
	71	5
...ion.	60	4
	14	1
...French	75	5
...ents	203	15
...s	29	2
	78	5
	136	9
	166	11
	45	3
...Afr.	167½	12
...ns	98	6
...as	152	10
	200	15
	16	1
	99	6
...byterian.		
	61	4
...eet	151	10
	126	8
	132	8
...Street	199	15
	185	14
	37	2
...reet	125	8
...reet	19	1
	193	14
...Street	92	6
	144	9
	17	1
	43	3
...h	76	5
...treet	81	5
...Street	53	3
	140	9
	88	6
	142	9
	111	7
	22	1
	97	6
...venue	162	11
...ree	92	6
	175	13
...treet	118	8
	196	14
	134	9

		Wards.
Methodist.		
First Episcopalian	27	
Second D.o	149	
Third D.o	67	
Fourth D.o	155	
Fifth D.o	178	
Sixth D.o	139	
Seventh D.o	165	
Eighth D.o	166½	
Ninth D.o	128	
Protestant Independant	122	
D.o D.o	173	
D.o D.o	190	
Primitive D.o	117	
D.o	160	
Independent	150	
Mariners D.o	59	
Asbury D.o African	194	
Zion D.o D.o	72	
Baptist.		
Abyssinian African	69	
Amity Street	202	
Bethel	121	
Bethel	156	
Bowne Street	179	
East	176	
Ebenezer	159	
First	26	
General	131	
Mott Street	194	
Mulberry Street	95	
Norfolk Street	172	
North	136	
Oliver Street	64	
South	31	
Union	157	
Welch	100	
Reformed Dutch.		
Bleecker Street	145	
Broome Street	127	
German	146	
Greene Street	130	
Mission	156	
Middle	24	
Ninth Street	205	
North	33	
North East	110	
North West	74	
South	10	
True	120	
Miscellaneous.		
Barrow Street Rom. Cath.	141	
Christ Church D.o	34	
St Marys D.o	174	
St Patricks D.o	197	
St Peters D.o	47	
Rose Street Friends	63	
Henry Street D.o	109	
Hester Street D.o	186	
Bleecker Street D.o	135	
First Unitarian	56	
Second Unitarian	129	
First Universalists	153	
United Friends D.o	91	
Independents	79	
Providence D.o	123	
St James Lutheran	187	
St Mathews D.o	107	
German Synagogue	152	
Portuguese D.o	5	
Mormon	52	
New Jerusalem	94	

REFERENCES TO BROOKLYN		Wards.
County Court House	1	3
Savings Bank	1	3
Apprentices Library	1	3
Long Island Bank	2	2
Brooklyn Fire Ins. Co.	3	2
Phenix D.o D.o	4	2
St Johns Episc. Church	5	2
St Johns D.o D.o	6	4
Presbyterian D.o	7	3
Baptist D.o	8	4
Methodist D.o	9	4
D.o D.o	10	5
D.o D.o African	11	4
Roman Cath. D.o	12	4
Street Com.ns Office	13	2
Market House	14	2
Public Gardens	15	
Hotels	16	

Illustration © David Rumsey Map Collection, www.davidrumsey.com

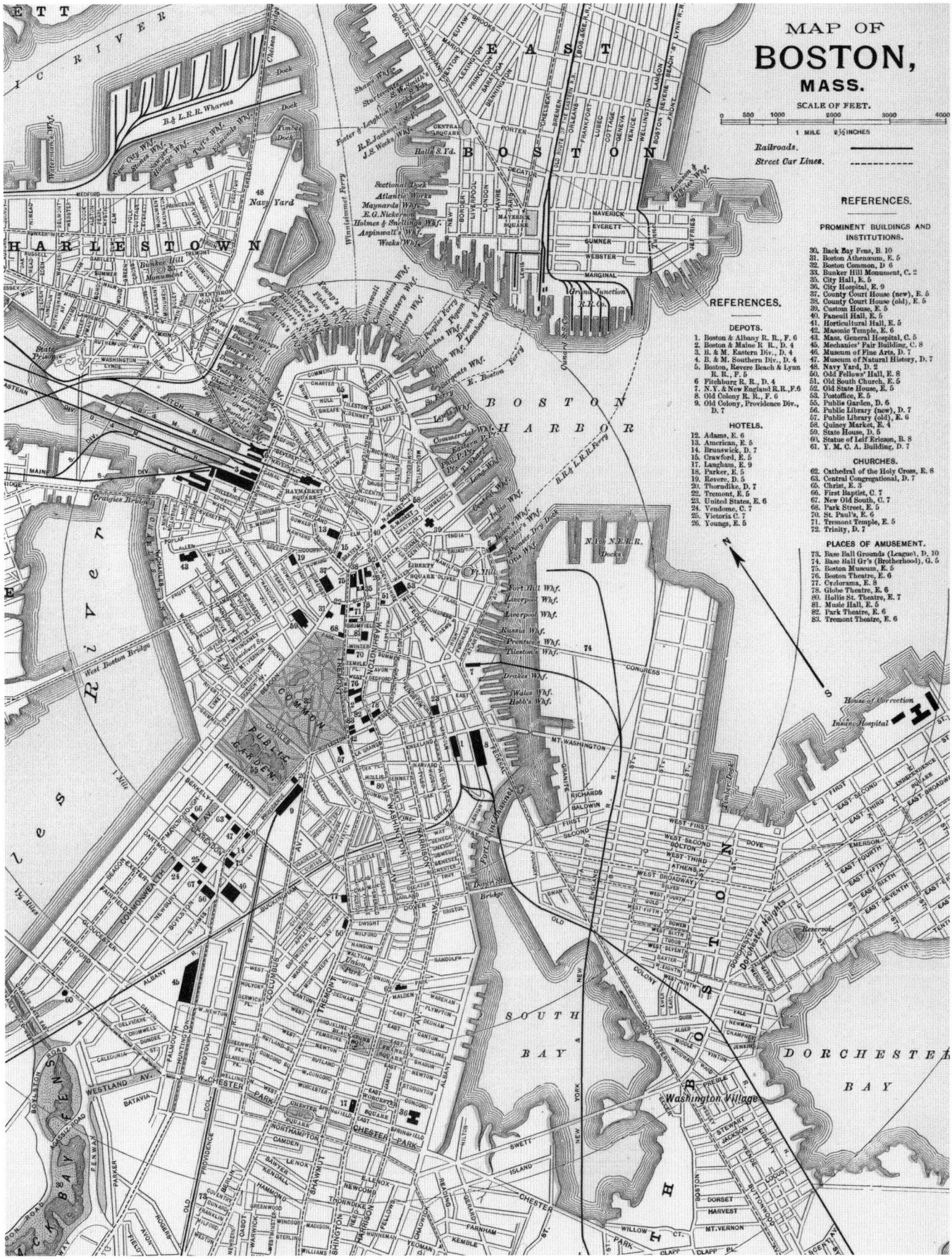
MAP OF
BOSTON,
MASS.
SCALE OF FEET.
0 500 1000 2000 3000 4000
1 MILE 2½ INCHES
Railroads.
Street Car Lines.
REFERENCES.
PROMINENT BUILDINGS AND INSTITUTIONS.
30. Back Bay Fens, B. 10
31. Boston Athenæum, E. 5
32. Boston Common, D 6
33. Bunker Hill Monument, C. 2
35. City Hall, E. 5
36. City Hospital, E. 9
37. County Court House (new), E. 5
38. County Court House (old), E. 5
39. Custom House, E. 5
40. Faneuil Hall, E. 5
41. Horticultural Hall, E. 5
42. Masonic Temple, E. 6
43. Mass. General Hospital, C. 5
45. Mechanics' Fair Building, C. 8
46. Museum of Fine Arts, D. 7
47. Museum of Natural History, D. 7
48. Navy Yard, D. 2
50. Old Fellows' Hall, E. 8
51. Old South Church, E. 5
52. Old State House, E. 5
53. Postoffice, E. 5
55. Public Garden, D. 6
56. Public Library (new), D. 7
57. Public Library (old), E. 6
58. Quincy Market, E. 4
59. State House, D. 5
60. Statue of Leif Ericson, B. 8
61. Y. M. C. A. Building, D. 7
CHURCHES.
62. Cathedral of the Holy Cross, E. 8
63. Central Congregational, D. 7
65. Christ, E. 3
66. First Baptist, C. 7
67. New Old South, C. 7
68. Park Street, E. 5
70. St. Paul's, E. 6
71. Tremont Temple, E. 5
72. Trinity, D. 7
PLACES OF AMUSEMENT.
73. Base Ball Grounds (League), D. 10
74. Base Ball Gr's (Brotherhood), G. 5
75. Boston Museum, E. 5
76. Boston Theatre, E. 6
77. Cyclorama, E. 8
78. Globe Theatre, E. 6
80. Hollis St. Theatre, E. 7
81. Music Hall, E. 5
82. Park Theatre, E. 6
83. Tremont Theatre, E. 6
REFERENCES.
DEPOTS.
1. Boston & Albany R. R., F. 6
2. Boston & Maine R. R., D. 4
3. B. & M. Eastern Div., D. 4
4. B. & M. Southern Div., D. 4
5. Boston, Revere Beach & Lynn R. R., F. 5
6 Fitchburg R. R., D. 4
7. N. Y. & New England R.R., F.6
8. Old Colony R. R., F. 6
9. Old Colony, Providence Div., D. 7
HOTELS.
12. Adams, E. 6
13. American, E. 5
14. Brunswick, D. 7
15. Crawford, E. 5
17. Langham, E. 9
18. Parker, E. 5
19. Revere, D. 5
20. Thorndike, D. 7
22. Tremont, E. 5
23. United States, E. 6
24. Vendome, C. 7
25. Victoria C. 7
26. Youngs, E. 5
EAST BOSTON
CHARLESTOWN
BOSTON HARBOR
SOUTH BOSTON
DORCHESTER BAY
BACK BAY FENS
Navy Yard
Bunker Hill Monument
Boston & Maine R.R.
Boston & Albany R.R.
Old Colony R.R.
Union Junction R.R.Co.
Eastern R.R.
Fitchburg R.R.
N.Y. N.H. & H.R.R.
Boston & Lowell R.R.
B.& L.R.R. Ferry
E. Boston Ferry
Charlestown Ferry
Chelsea Ferry
Cunard S.S.Co.
Cragie's Bridge
West Boston Bridge
Dorchester Bridge
Washington Village
Reservoir
House of Correction
Insane Hospital
Navy Yard
Dry Dock
Charles River
Mystic River
Back Bay
Boston Harbor
Dorchester Bay
Boston Common
Public Garden
Washington St.
Tremont St.
Boylston St.
Commonwealth Av.
Beacon St.
Cambridge St.
Charles St.
Cambridge St.
Washington St.
Tremont St.
Boylston St.
Commonwealth Av.
Beacon St.
Cambridge St.
Charles

Illustration © David Rumsey Map Collection, www.davidrumsey.com

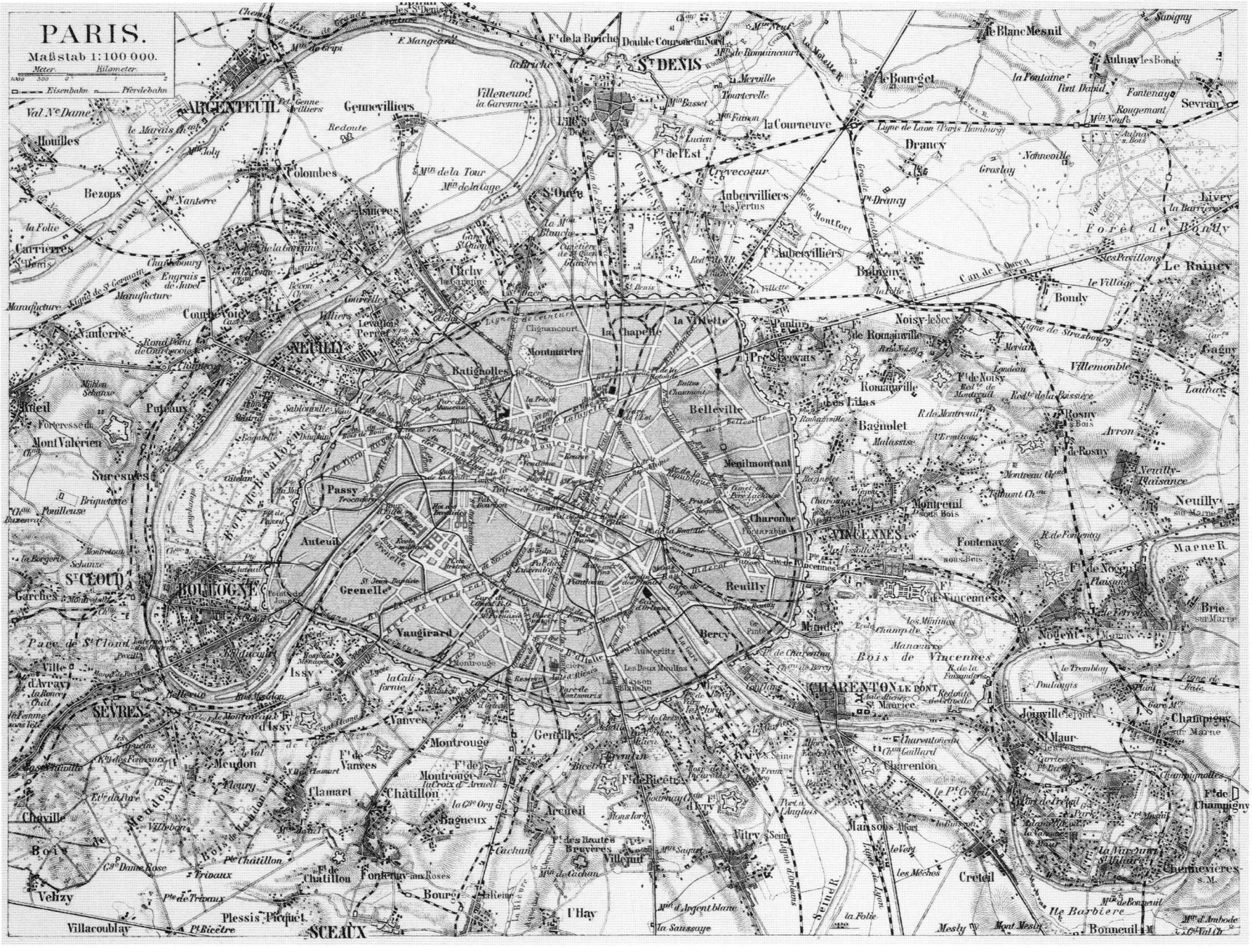
PARIS.
Maßstab 1:100 000.
Meter
Kilometer
Eisenbahn
Pferdebahn
ARGENTEUIL
Gennevilliers
Villeneuve la Garenne
St DENIS
Le Blanc Mesnil
Le Bourget
Aulnay les Bondy
Sevran
Drancy
Aubervilliers
Pantin
Bobigny
Le Raincy
Bondy
Noisy-le-Sec
Romainville
Les Lilas
Bagnolet
Montreuil
Vincennes
Fontenay
Nogent
Joinville le Pont
St Maur
Charenton
Ivry
Vitry
Maisons Alfort
Créteil
Bonneuil
Villejuif
Gentilly
Arcueil
Bagneux
Montrouge
Vanves
Issy
Vaugirard
Grenelle
Auteuil
Passy
Batignolles
Montmartre
Belleville
Ménilmontant
Charonne
Reuilly
Bercy
Bois de Vincennes
Bois de Boulogne
Neuilly
Puteaux
Suresnes
Mont Valérien
Bezons
Colombes
Asnières
Clichy
Levallois Perret
Courbevoie
Nanterre
Rueil
Garches
St Cloud
Meudon
Sèvres
Clamart
Châtillon
Fontenay aux Roses
Bourg la Reine
Plessis Piquet
Villacoublay
SCEAUX
Velizy
Chaville
Vincennes
Nogent
Champigny
Chennevières s. M.
Brie sur Marne
Neuilly-Plaisance
Livry
Gagny
Villemomble
Le Raincy
Forêt de Bondy
Bois de Vincennes
Bois de Boulogne
Seine R.
Marne R.
Ligne de Strasbourg
Ligne de Laon (Paris Hamburg)
Ligne de Ceinture
Ligne d'Orléans
Ligne de Sceaux
Canal de l'Ourcq
Canal St Denis
Canal St Ouen
Canal St Denis
Canal St Maur
Canal St Ouen
Canal St Denis
Canal St Ouen
Canal St Denis
Canal St Ouen
Canal St Denis

Illustration © GettyImages.com/THEPALMER

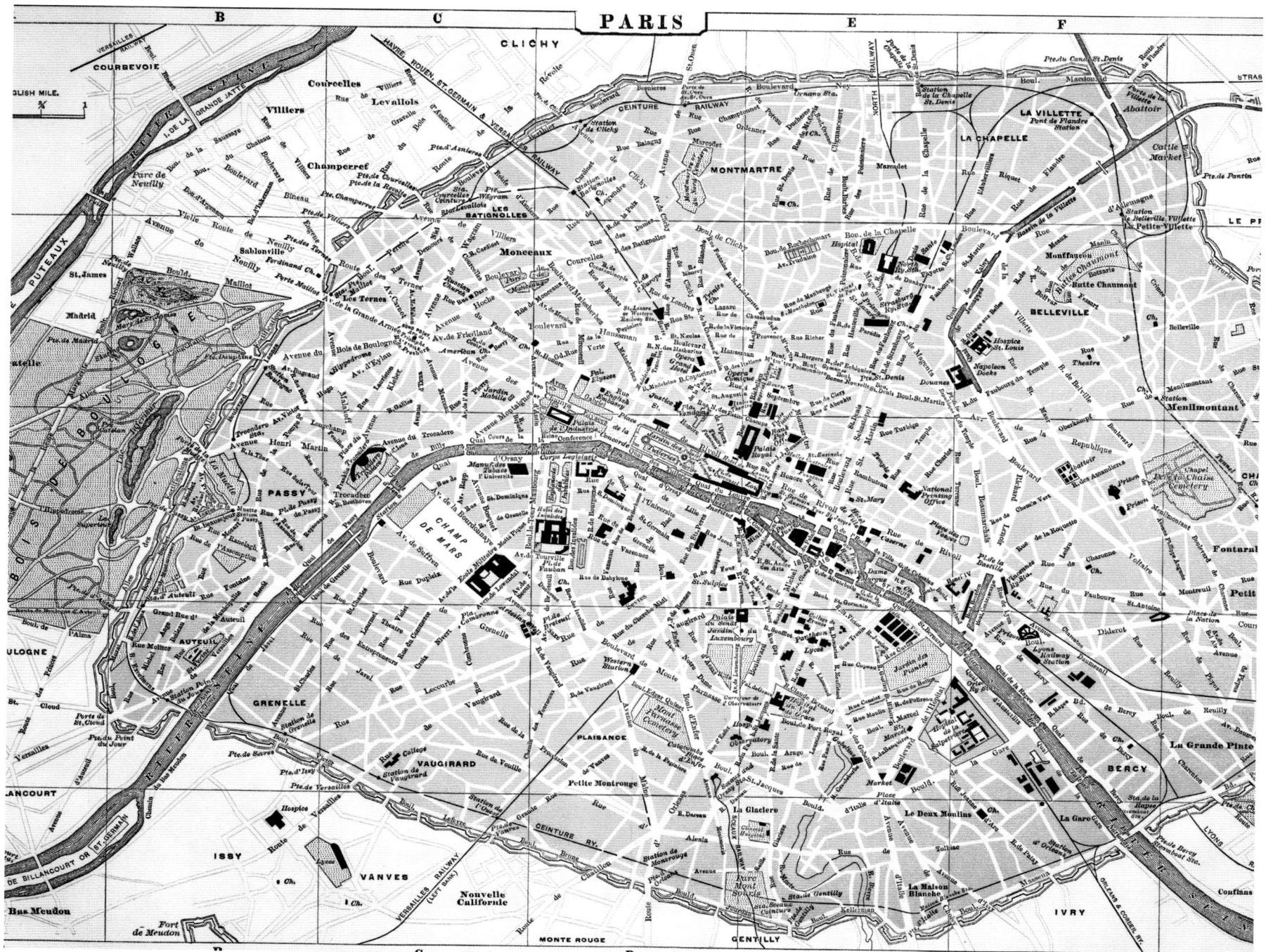
PARIS
B
C
E
F
CLICHY
COURBEVOIE
Courcelles
Villiers
Levallois
Champerret
Parc de Neuilly
Monceaux
MONTMARTRE
LA CHAPELLE
LA VILLETTE
Pont de Flandre Station
Abattoir
Cattle Market
BELLEVILLE
Butte Chaumont
Menilmontant
Napoleon Docks
Hospice St. Louis
Pere la Chaise Cemetery
Fontarai
Petit
La Grande Pinte
BERCY
La Garc
Le Deux Moulins
La Maison Blanche
IVRY
GENTILLY
MONTE ROUGE
Nouvelle Californie
VANVES
ISSY
Bas Meudon
Fort de Meudon
LANCOURT
GRENELLE
VAUGIRARD
AUTEUIL
PASSY
CHAMP DE MARS
PLAISANCE
Petite Montrouge
La Glaciere
Parc Mont Sourris
Observatory
Mont Parnasse Cemetery
Jardin du Luxembourg
Palais du Senat
Palais du Jardin des Plantes
Hôtel des Invalides
Palais de l'Industrie
Palais de la Conference
Jardin des Tuileries
Palais Royal
Palais de Justice
Hôtel de Ville
Bastille
Gare de Lyon
Gare de Bercy
Gare d'Orsay
Gare de Montparnasse
Gare du Nord
Gare de Lyon
Gare de Vaugirard
Gare de Grenelle
Gare de Monrouge
Gare de Gentilly
Gare de Bercy
Gare de Lyon
Gare de Vincennes
Gare de Versailles
Gare de Clichy
Gare de Batignolles
Gare de Courcelles
Gare de Levallois
Gare de Neuilly
Gare de Passy
Gare de Auteuil
Gare de Grenelle
Gare de Vaugirard
Gare de Mont

Illustration © GettyImages.com/THEPALMER

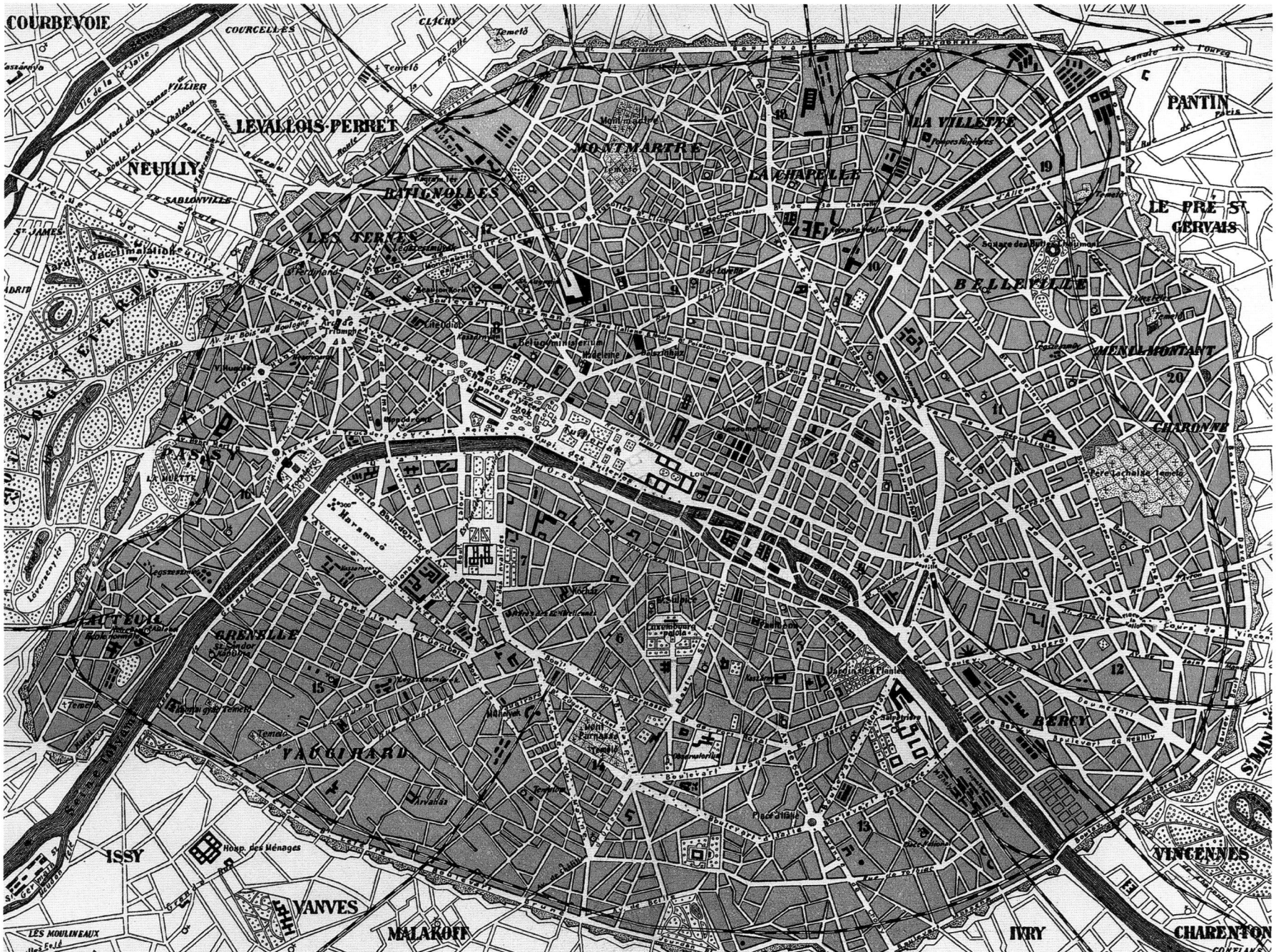
COURBEVOIE
COURCELLES
CLICHY
LEVALLOIS-PERRET
NEUILLY
BATIGNOLLES
MONTMARTRE
LA CHAPELLE
LA VILLETTE
PANTIN
LE PRE ST. GERVAIS
BELLEVILLE
MENILMONTANT
CHARONNE
LES TERNES
PASSY
CHAILLOT
GRENELLE
VAUGIRARD
BERCY
ISSY
VANVES
MALAKOFF
IVRY
VINCENNES
CHARENTON
Hôp. des Ménages
Marsmeré
Arc de Triomphe
Luxembourg
Palais
Place d'Italie
Jardin des Plantes
Père Lachaise
Temple
Arsenal
Sablonville
Ste. James
Les Moulineaux
Conflans

Illustration © GettyImages.com/Nastasic

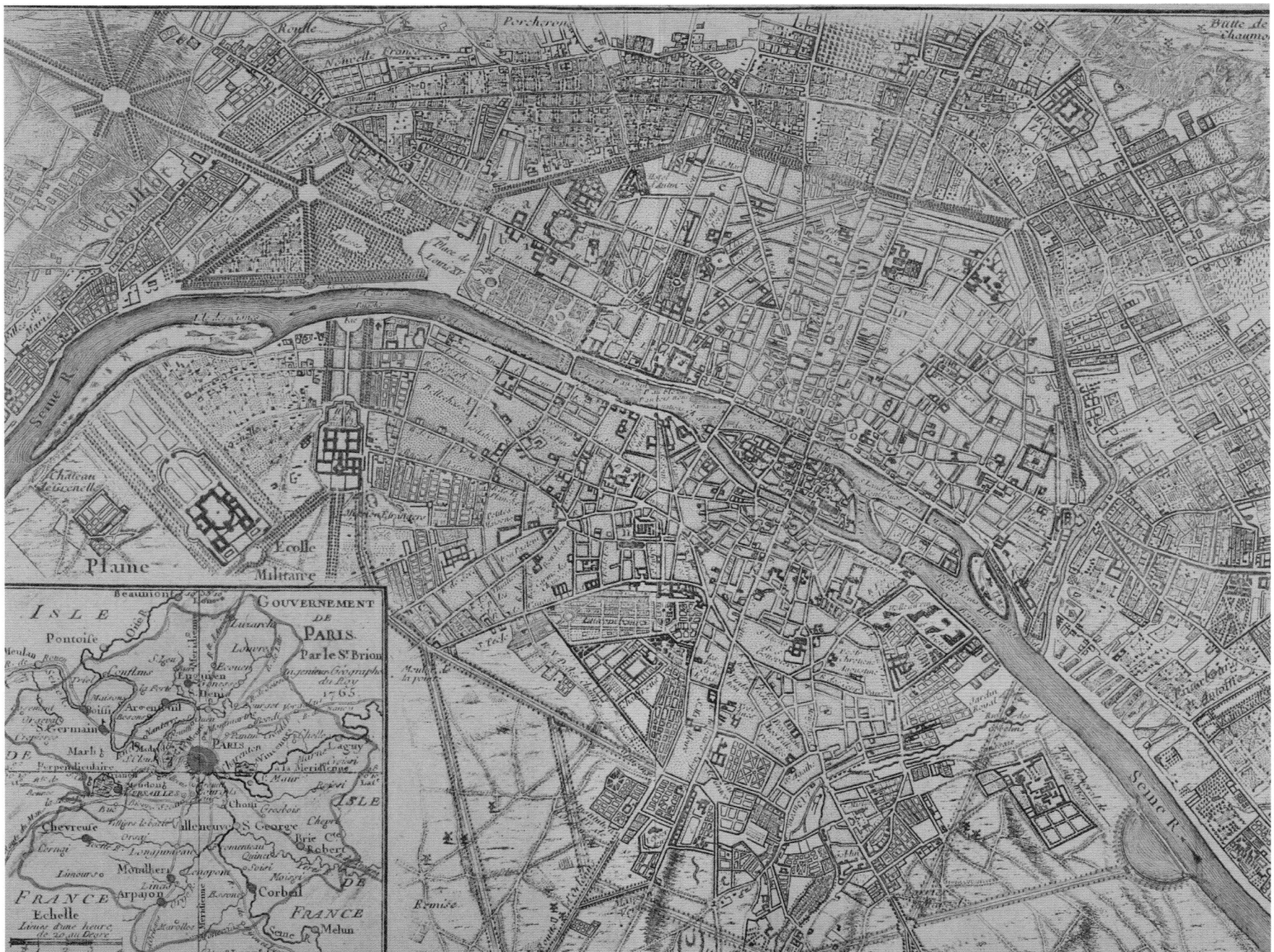
Porcheron
Butte de Chaumo
Place de Louis XV
Seine R.
Plaine
Ecolle
Militaire
Ermise
Seine R.
GOUVERNEMENT DE PARIS.
Par le Sr. Brion
Ingenieur Geographe du Roy
1765
ISLE
DE
FRANCE
Beaumont
Pontoise
Meulan
Conflans
Enghien
Poissy
St Germain
Marly
Paris
Lagny
Perpendiculaire
Meudon
Versailles
Choisy
Chevreuse
Villeneuve
S. George
Brie Comte Robert
Longjumeau
Montlhery
Corbeil
Arpajon
Echelle
Lieues d'une heure de 20 au Degre
Melun
Seine R.

Illustration © GettyImages.com/Hemera Technologies

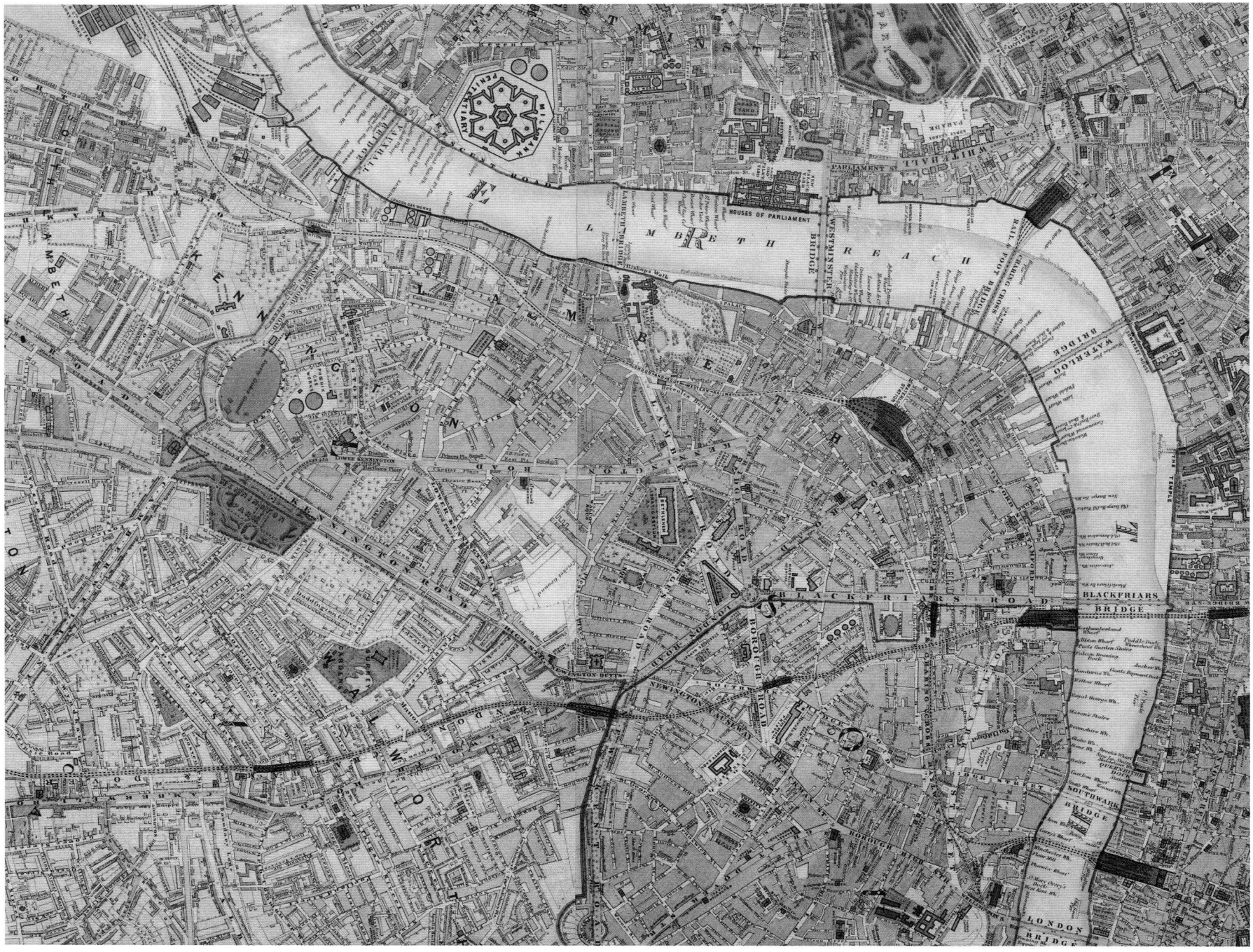
HOUSES OF PARLIAMENT
WESTMINSTER BRIDGE
LAMBETH REACH
WATERLOO BRIDGE
BLACKFRIARS BRIDGE
SOUTHWARK BRIDGE
LONDON BRIDGE
BLACKFRIARS ROAD
BOROUGH ROAD
NEWINGTON BUTTS
KENNINGTON ROAD
LAMBETH
WESTMINSTER
PARLIAMENT
WHITEHALL
PENITENTIARY
MILLBANK
VAUXHALL
LOWER KENNINGTON
Abingdon St.
Bishops Walk
Princes Pl. Regent
Kennington Oval
Kennington Cross
Kennington Lane
Kennington Road
Lambeth Bridge
Lambeth Palace
Lambeth Road
Lambeth Walk
Lambeth Wharf
Lambeth Pier
Lambeth Terrace
Lambeth Cut
Lambeth Church
Lambeth Hospital
Lambeth Workhouse
Lambeth Place

Illustration © David Rumsey Map Collection, www.davidrumsey.com

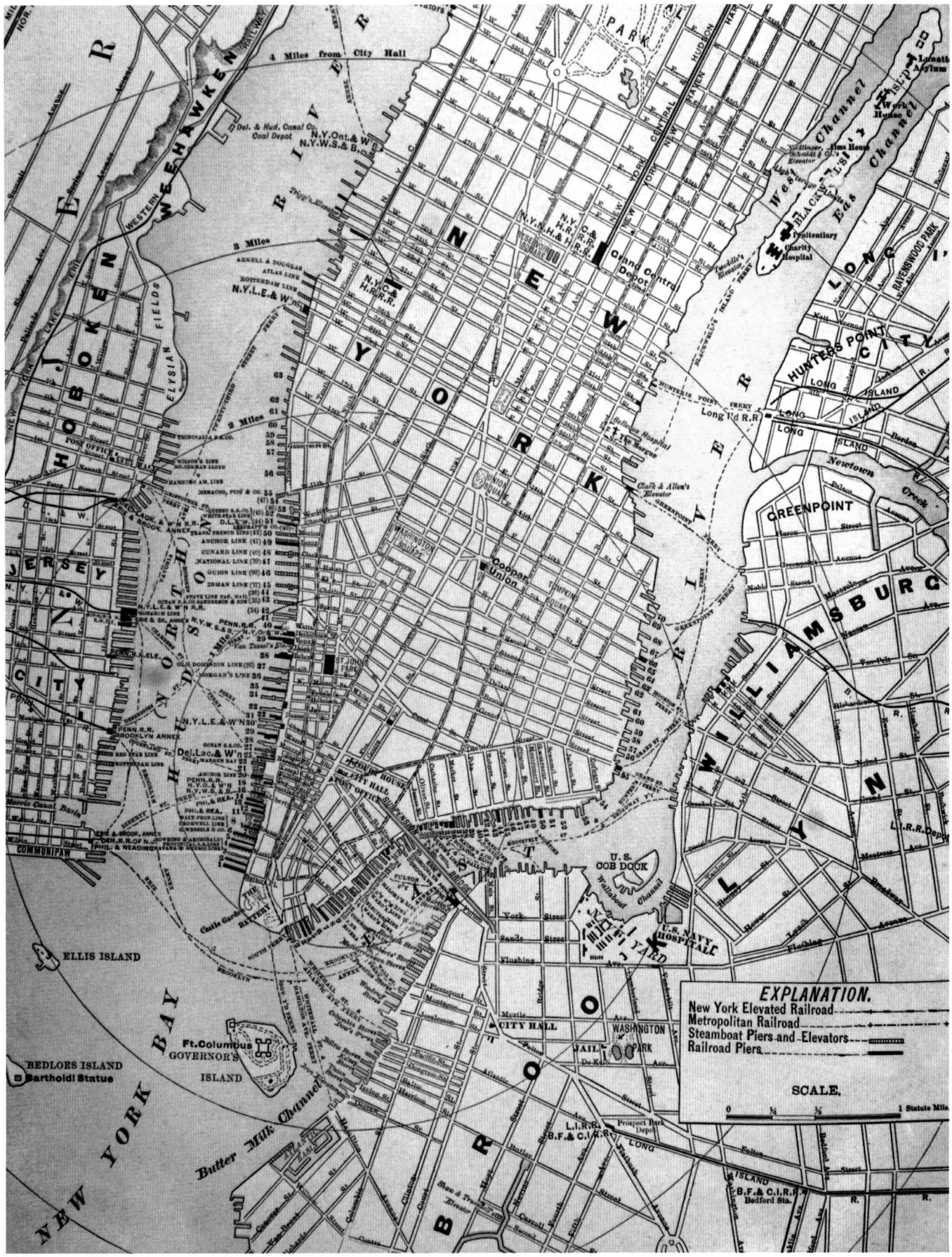
EXPLANATION.
New York Elevated Railroad
Metropolitan Railroad
Steamboat Piers and Elevators
Railroad Piers
SCALE.
0 ¼ ½ 1 Statute Mile
HOBOKEN
WEEHAWKEN
JERSEY CITY
HUDSON RIVER
NEW YORK
EAST RIVER
LONG ISLAND CITY
WILLIAMSBURG
BROOKLYN
NEW YORK BAY
ELLIS ISLAND
Ft. Columbus
GOVERNOR'S ISLAND
BEDLOES ISLAND
Bartholdi Statue
Butter Milk Channel
Grand Central Depot
Cooper Union
U.S. COB DOCK
U.S. NAVY HOSPITAL
CITY HALL
WASHINGTON PARK
GREENPOINT
HUNTERS POINT
Newtown Creek
Long Island R.R.
Del. & Hud. Canal Co. Coal Depot
N.Y.Ont.& W.
N.Y.W.S.& B.
N.Y.L.E.& W'ns
Del.Lac.& W'ns
Penitentiary
Charity Hospital
Bellevue Hospital
Morris Canal Basin
COMMUNIPAW
Castle Garden
BATTERY
Prospect Park Depot
L.I.R.R.
B.F.& C.I.R.R.
Bedford Sta.
Flushing
Fulton
Myrtle
Atlantic
Pacific
Bridge
Broadway
Lexington
Madison
Fifth
Sixth
Seventh
Eighth
Ninth
Tenth
Eleventh
Seventh Street
Ninth Street
Tenth Street
Eleventh Street
Seventh Avenue
Ninth Avenue
Tenth Avenue
Eleventh Avenue
Seventh Street
Ninth Street
Tenth Street
Eleventh Street
Seventh Avenue
Ninth Avenue
Tenth Avenue
Eleventh Avenue

Illustration © Shutterstock.com/I. Pilon

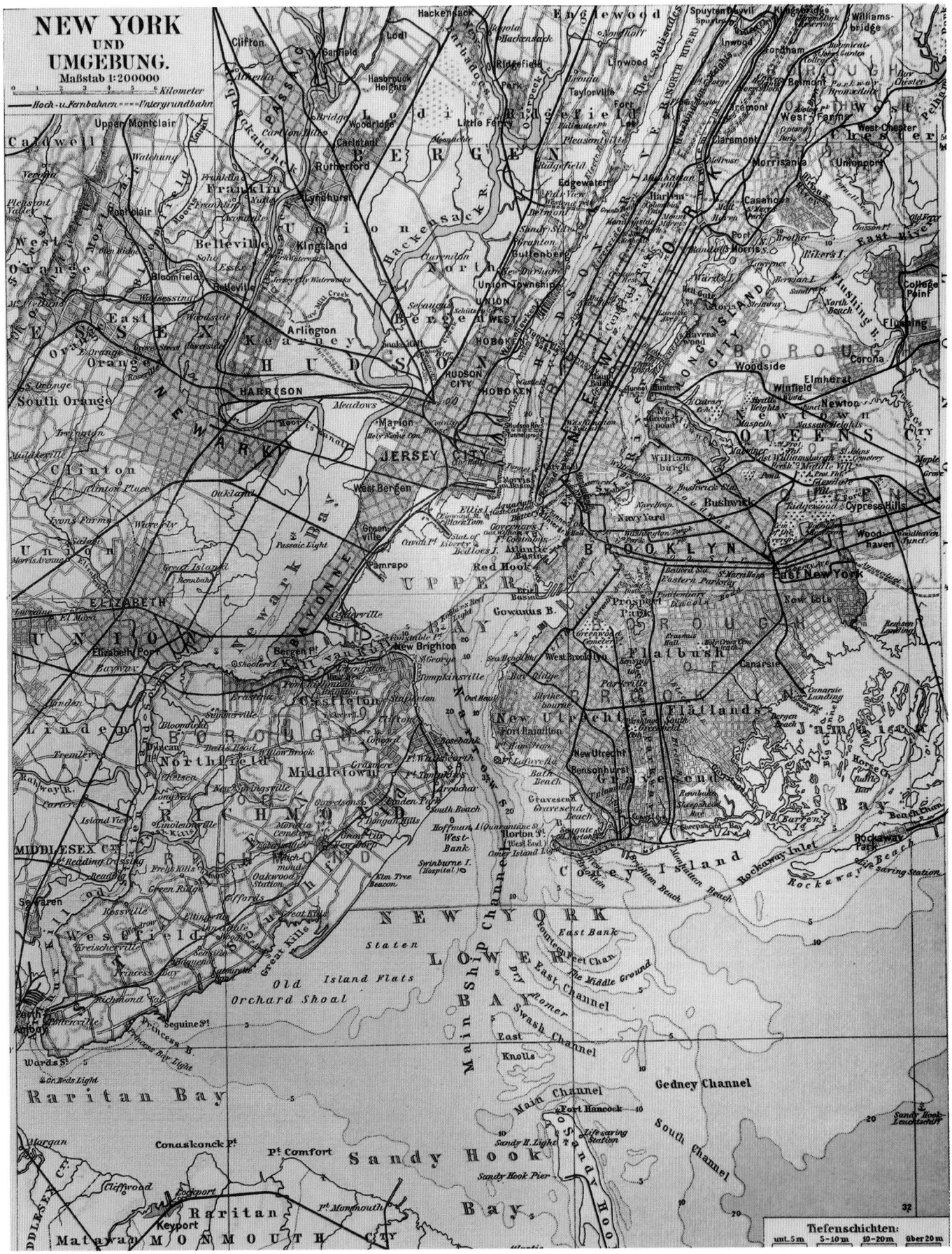
NEW YORK
UND
UMGEBUNG.
Maßstab 1:200000
0 1 2 3 4 5 6 Kilometer
Hoch- u. Fernbahnen
Untergrundbahn
Hackensack
Englewood
Clifton
Garfield
Lodi
Ridgefield
Hasbrouck Heights
Teaneck
Paterson
Passaic
Upper Montclair
Caldwell
Bloomfield
Belleville
Kearney
Arlington
Harrison
Hoboken
Jersey City
Newark
Elizabeth
Elizabeth Port
Bayonne
Staten Island
Brooklyn
Flatbush
Flatlands
Jamaica
Queens
Long Island City
Flushing
Corona
Woodside
Elmhurst
Newton
Williamsburg
Bushwick
East New York
Cypress Hills
Woodhaven
Rockaway Beach
Coney Island
Gravesend
New Utrecht
Bensonhurst
Bay Ridge
Red Hook
Gowanus B.
Prospect Park
Canarsie
Rockaway Inlet
Sandy Hook
Sandy Hook Bay
Raritan Bay
Raritan
Keyport
Matawan
Conaskonck Pt.
Pt. Comfort
Pt. Monmouth
Cliffwood
Morgan
Perth Amboy
Staten Island
Old Orchard Shoal
Island Flats
Main Ship Channel
Swash Channel
Gedney Channel
Main Channel
South Channel
Fort Hancock
Sandy Hook Pier
Tiefenschichten:
unt. 5 m
5-10 m
10-20 m
über 20 m

Illustration © Shutterstock.com/Nicku

PRAG.

Maßstab 1:27.000

1000 Meter oder 1 Kilometer.

0 — 500 — 1000

Mariensäule	E2	9 Ehem. israel. Raths.	D2
Altst. Brückenturm	D2	10 Handelsakademie	E2
Karls IV. Monument	D2	11 Münzamt	D2
Nepomuk	C2	12 Finanzprokuratur	D2
Franzens Monum.[t]	D3	13 Finanz Landes Direkt.	F2
Radetzky "	C2	14 Schlick Palast	D3
Jungmann "	E3	15 D. Mädchen Lyceum	E3
Oberlandesgericht	C2	16 Naturwiss. Institut	E4

17 Städt. Markthalle E 3.

——— Straßenbahn.

PRAG UND UMGEBUNG.

Maßstab 1:70.000

0 — ½ — 1 — 2 Kilometer

——— Straßenbahn.

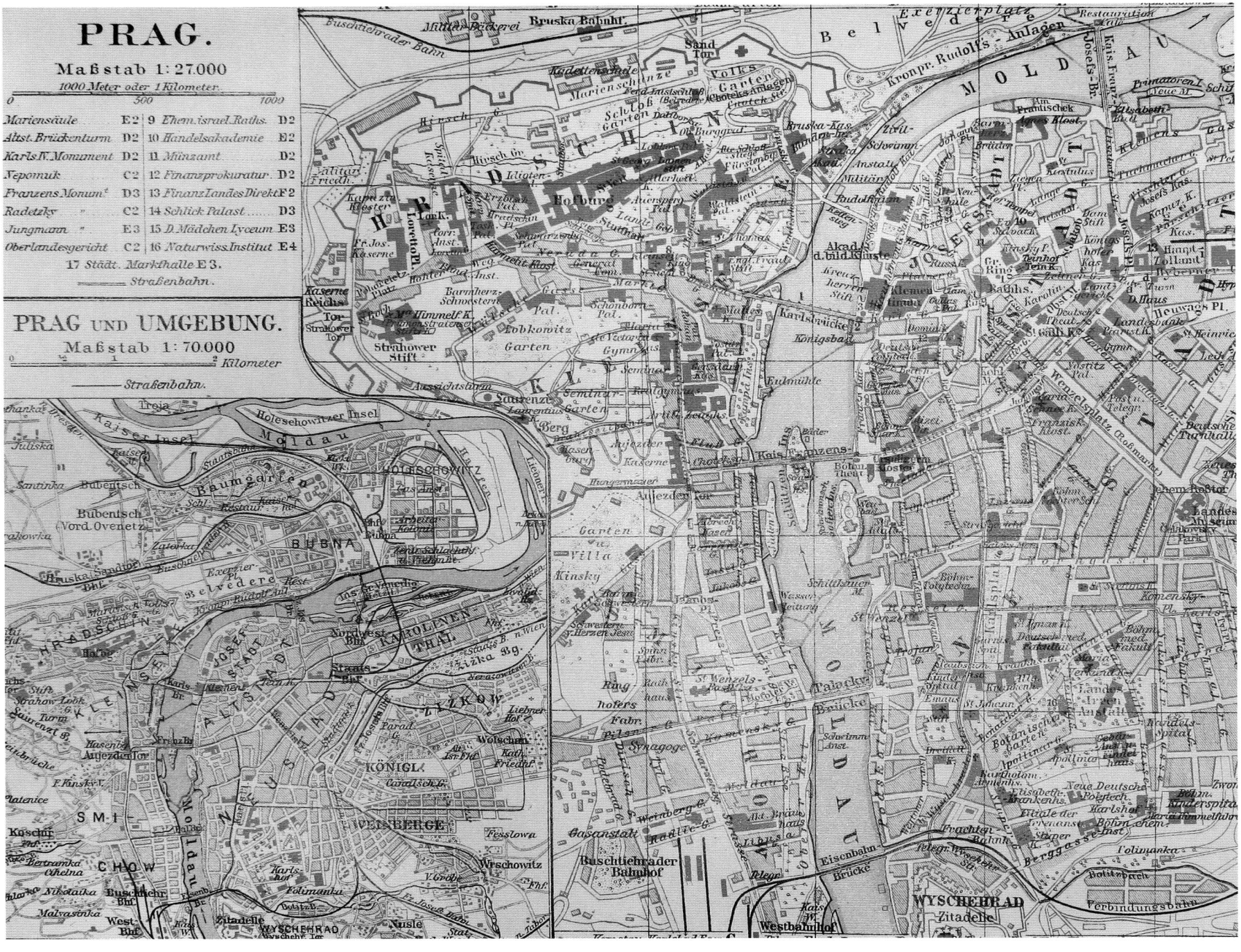

Illustration © Shutterstock.com/Nicku

KOPENHAGEN.

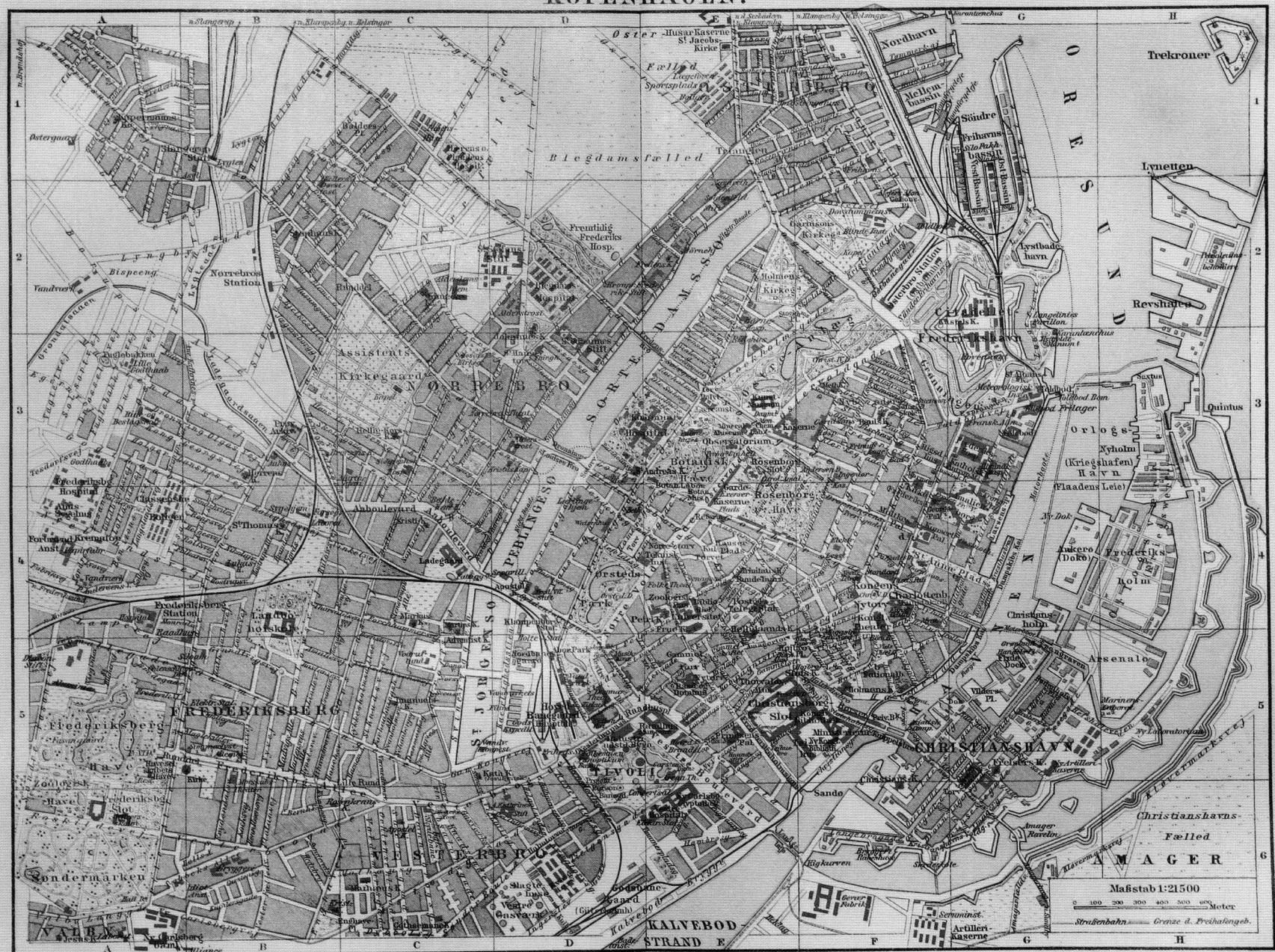

Meyers Konv.-Lexikon, 6. Aufl.

Bibliographisches Institut in Leipzig

Zum Artikel „Kopenhagen".

Illustration © Shutterstock.com/Nicku

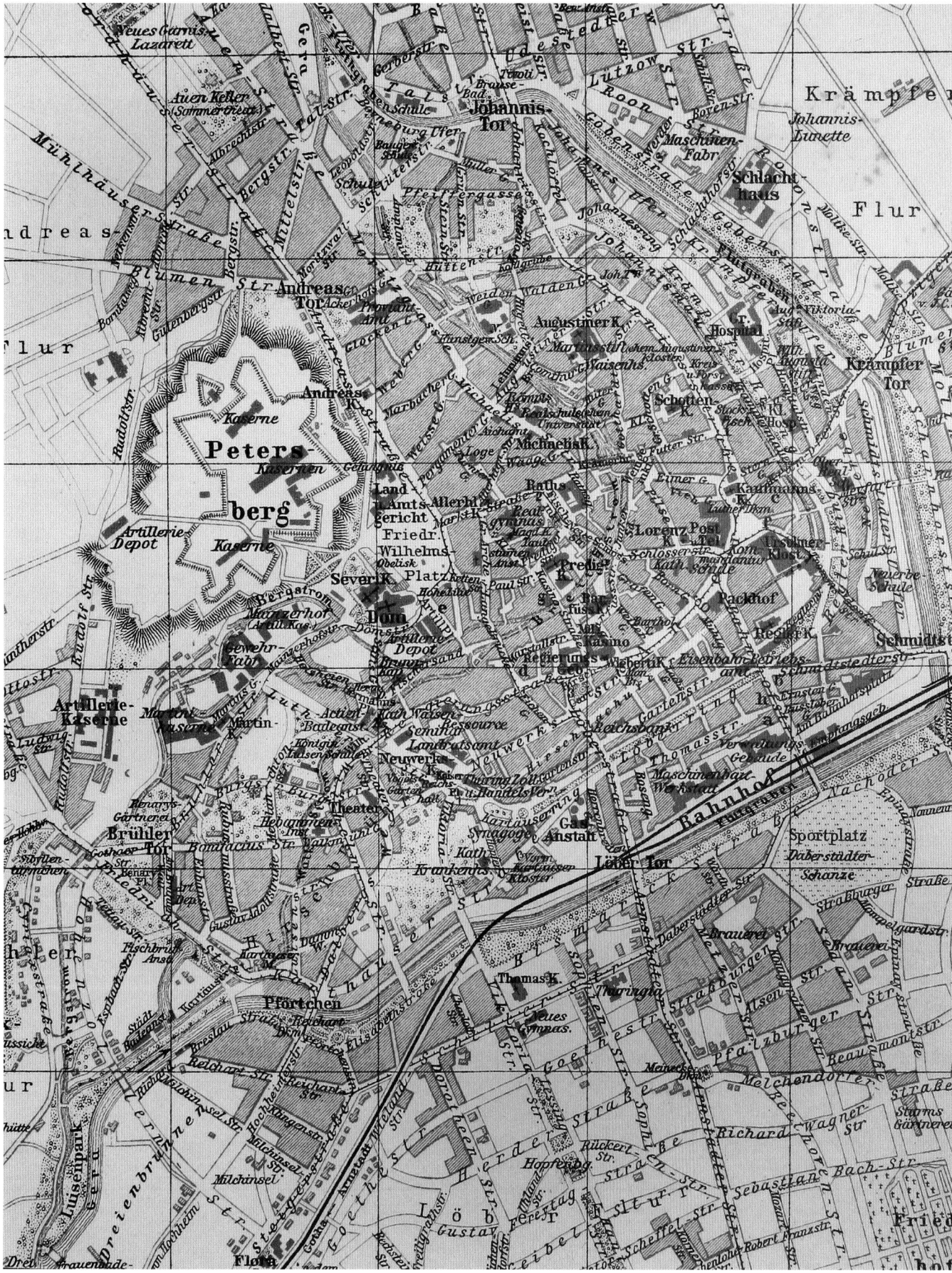
Neues Garnis-Lazarett
Auen Keller (Sommertreat.)
Johannis-Tor
Johannis-Lunette
Krämpfer
Flur
Maschinen-Fabr.
Schlacht-haus
Andreas-Tor
Andreas-K.
Kaserne
Peters-berg
Kasernen
Artillerie-Depot
Augustiner K.
Hospital
Krämpfer Tor
Schotten-K.
Michaelis K.
Land-Amts-gericht
Friedr. Wilhelms-Platz
Severi K.
Dom
Lorenz Post
Ursuliner Klost.
Pred.-K.
Packhof
Regier.-K.
Schmidtste
Bergstrom
Mauzerhof
Gewehr-Fabr.
Artillerie-Kaserne
Martin-K.
Kasino
Reichsbank
Neuwerks-K.
Landratsamt
Theater
Brühler Tor
Bahnhof
Sportplatz
Löber Tor
Synagoge
Gas-Anstalt
Thomas K.
Thuringia
Neues Gymnas.
Pförtchen
Luisenpark
Flora
Löbr
Friedr

Illustration © Shutterstock.com/Nicku

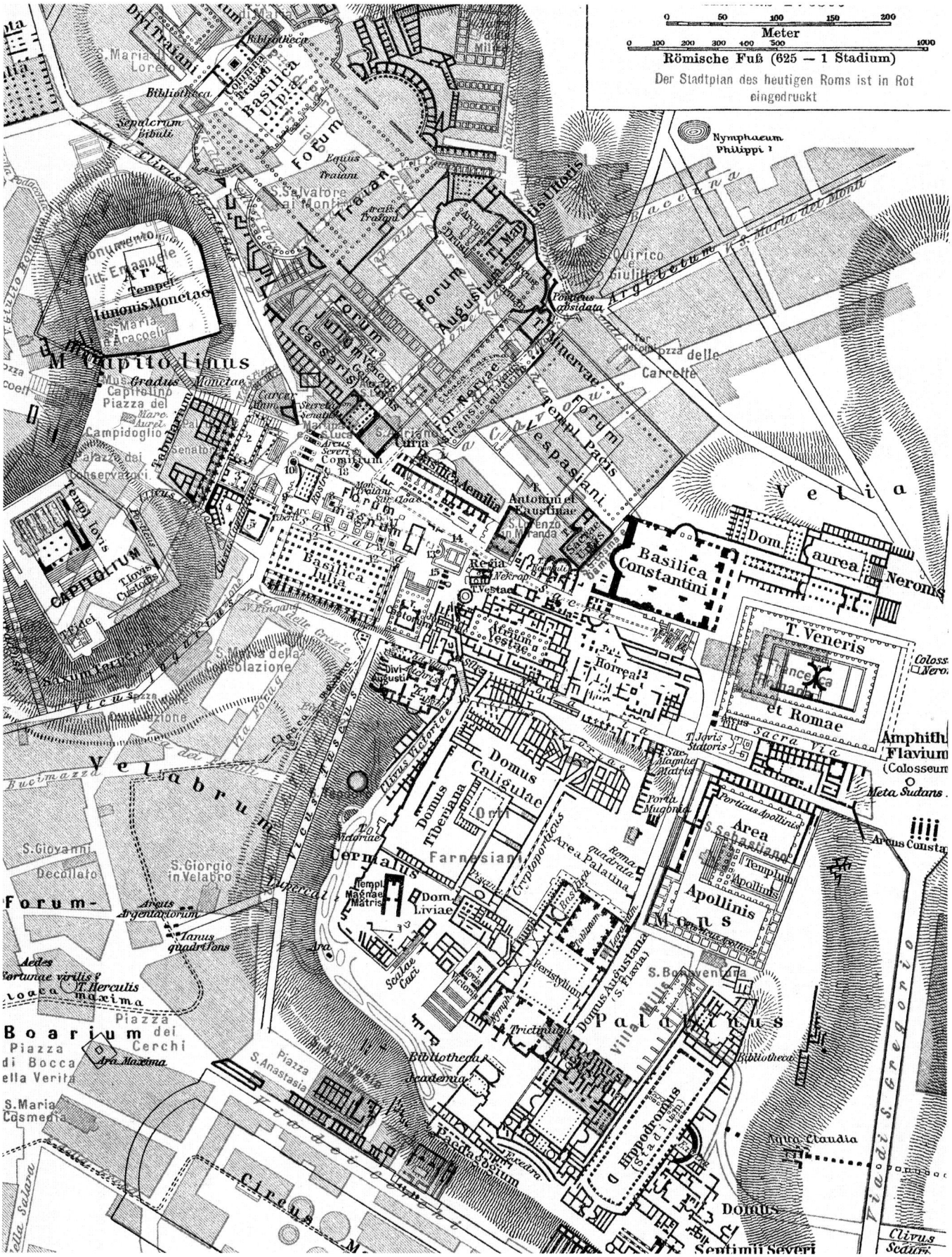
0 50 100 150 200
Meter
0 100 200 300 400 500 1000
Römische Fuß (625 — 1 Stadium)
Der Stadtplan des heutigen Roms ist in Rot eingedruckt
Nymphaeum Philippi ?
Bibliotheca
Basilica Ulpia
Forum Traiani
Sepulcrum Tibuli
Clivus Capitolinus
Arx
Templ. Iunonis Monetae
Mons Capitolinus
Gradus Monetae
Piazza del Campidoglio
Palazzo dei Conservatori
Tabularium
Templ. Iovis
Capitolium
Forum Augusti
Forum Caesaris
Forum Nervae
Forum Vespasiani
Templ. Pacis
Curia
Basilica Aemilia
Forum Romanum
Basilica Iulia
Regia
Vestae
Basilica Constantini
Domus aurea Neronis
T. Veneris et Romae
Amphitheatrum Flavium (Colosseum)
Meta Sudans
Arcus Constantini
Via sacra
Horreum
Domus Caligulae
Domus Tiberiana
Farnesiani
Area Palatina
Area Apollinis
Templum Apollinis
Palatinus
Domus Augustana
Hippodromus
Bibliotheca
Aqua Claudia
Domus Septimii Severi
Clivus Scauri
Circus Maximus
Forum Boarium
Piazza dei Cerchi
Ara Maxima
Aedes Fortunae virilis ?
T. Herculis maxima
Arcus Argentariorum
Janus quadrifrons
Velabrum
S. Giovanni Decollato
S. Giorgio in Velabro
Cermalus
Templ. Magnae Matris
Dom. Liviae
Scalae Caci
Ara
Bibliotheca
Academia
Piazza S. Anastasia
S. Maria Cosmedin
Piazza della Consolazione
Via Latina
Via Sacra
Via Nova
Via Latina

Illustration © Shutterstock.com/Sergey Kohl

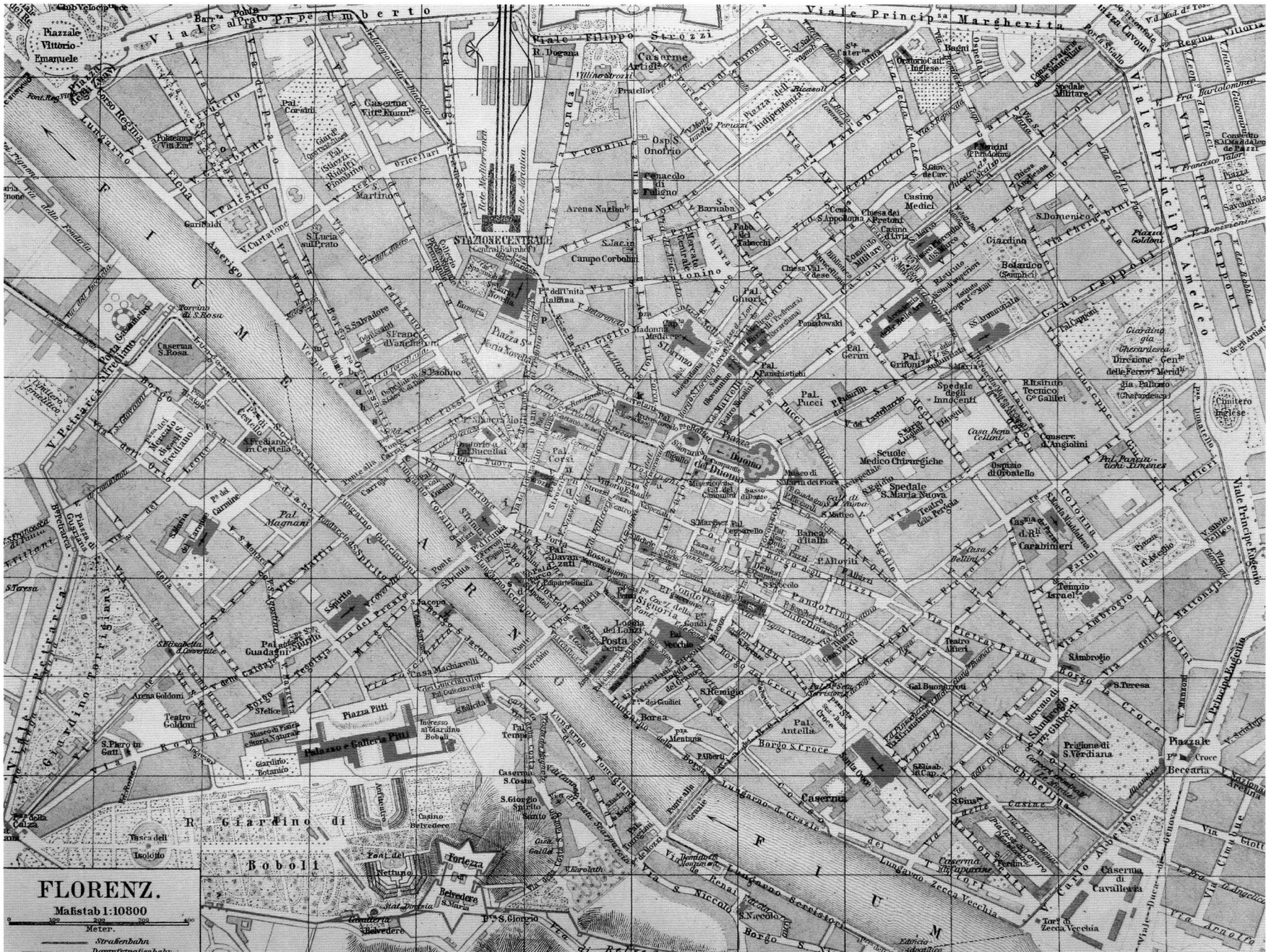
FLORENZ.
Maßstab 1:10800
0 100 200 300 400
Meter.
Straßenbahn
Dampfstraßenbahn
STAZIONE CENTRALE
Viale Principe Amedeo
Viale Principessa Margherita
Viale Filippo Strozzi
Viale al Prato
Lungarno
Via Nazionale
Via Cerretani
Via Calzaiuoli
Via Tornabuoni
Via Rondinelli
Via Ghibellina
Via Cavour
Via Ricasoli
Via Cerretani
Via Pecori
Via Ginori
Via Cavour
Via Ghibellina
Via Nazionale
Via Rondinelli
Via Tornabuoni
Via Calzaiuoli

Illustration © Shutterstock.com/Nicku

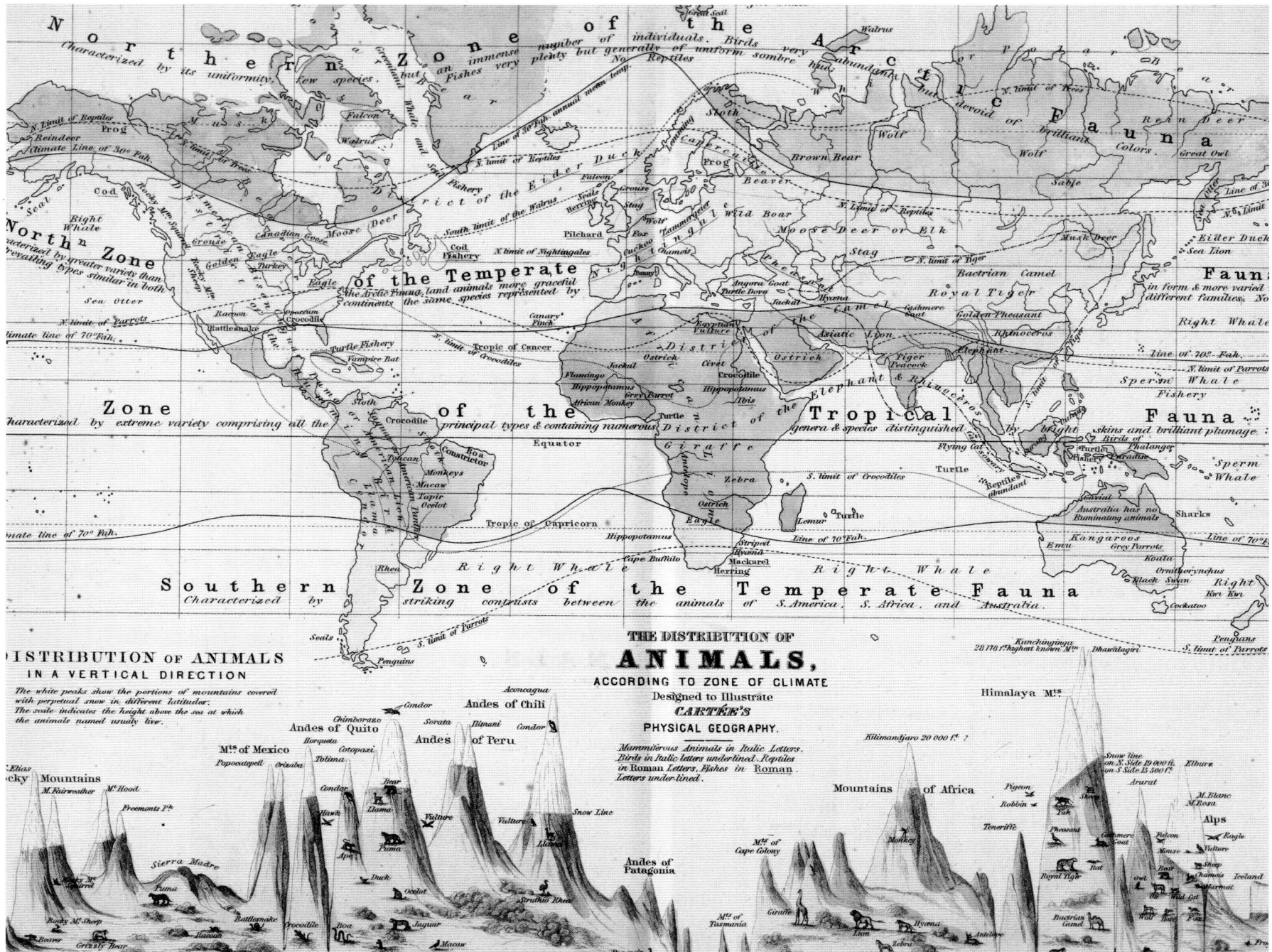

DISTRIBUTION OF ANIMALS
IN A VERTICAL DIRECTION

The white peaks show the portions of mountains covered with perpetual snow in different latitudes. The scale indicates the height above the sea at which the animals named usually live.

Illustration © David Rumsey Map Collection, www.davidrumsey.com

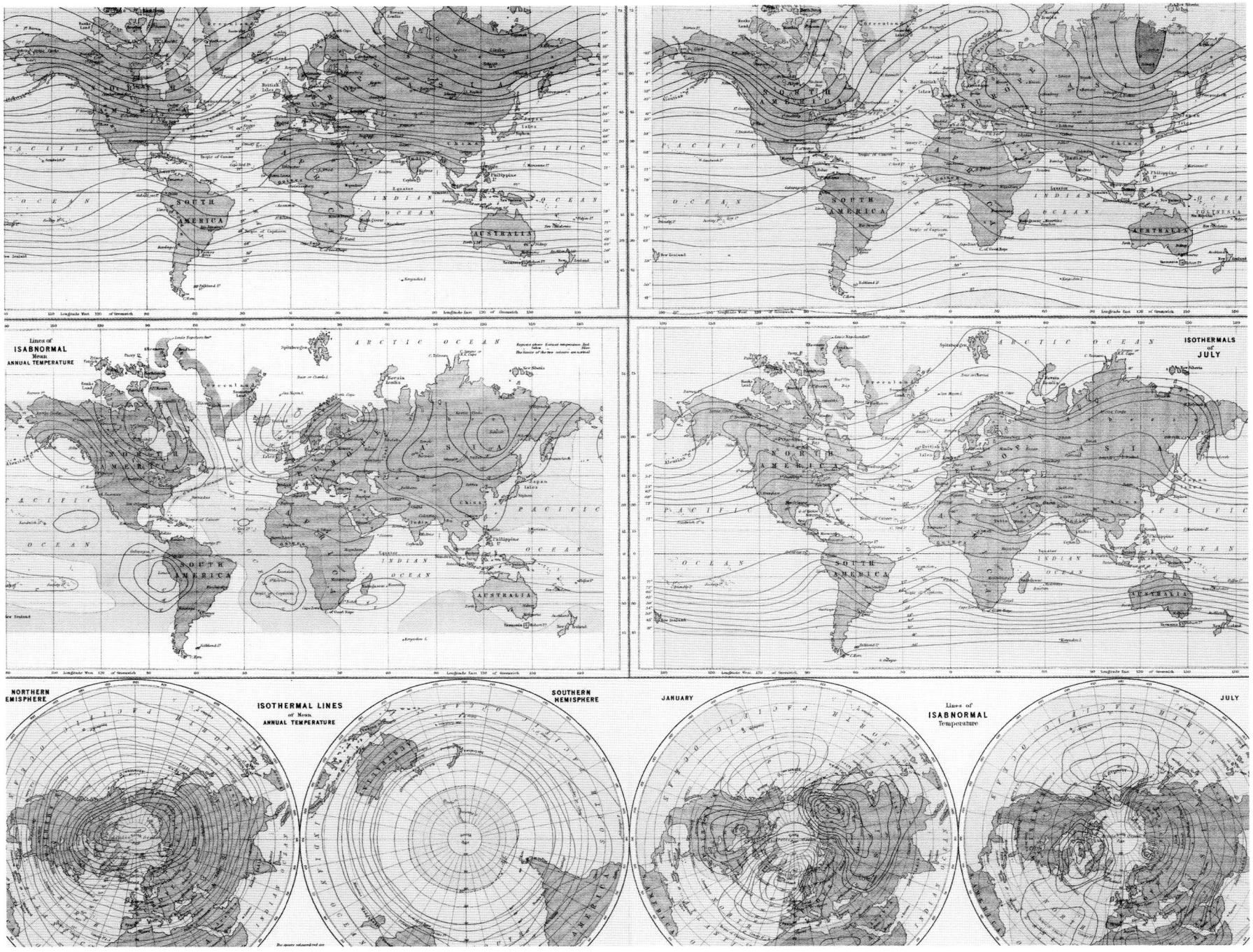
Lines of
ISABNORMAL
Mean
ANNUAL TEMPERATURE
ISOTHERMALS
of
JULY
NORTHERN
HEMISPHERE
ISOTHERMAL LINES
of Mean
ANNUAL TEMPERATURE
SOUTHERN
HEMISPHERE
JANUARY
Lines of
ISABNORMAL
Temperature
JULY
ARCTIC OCEAN
NORTH AMERICA
SOUTH AMERICA
AUSTRALIA
ASIA
PACIFIC OCEAN
INDIAN OCEAN

Illustration © David Rumsey Map Collection, www.davidrumsey.com

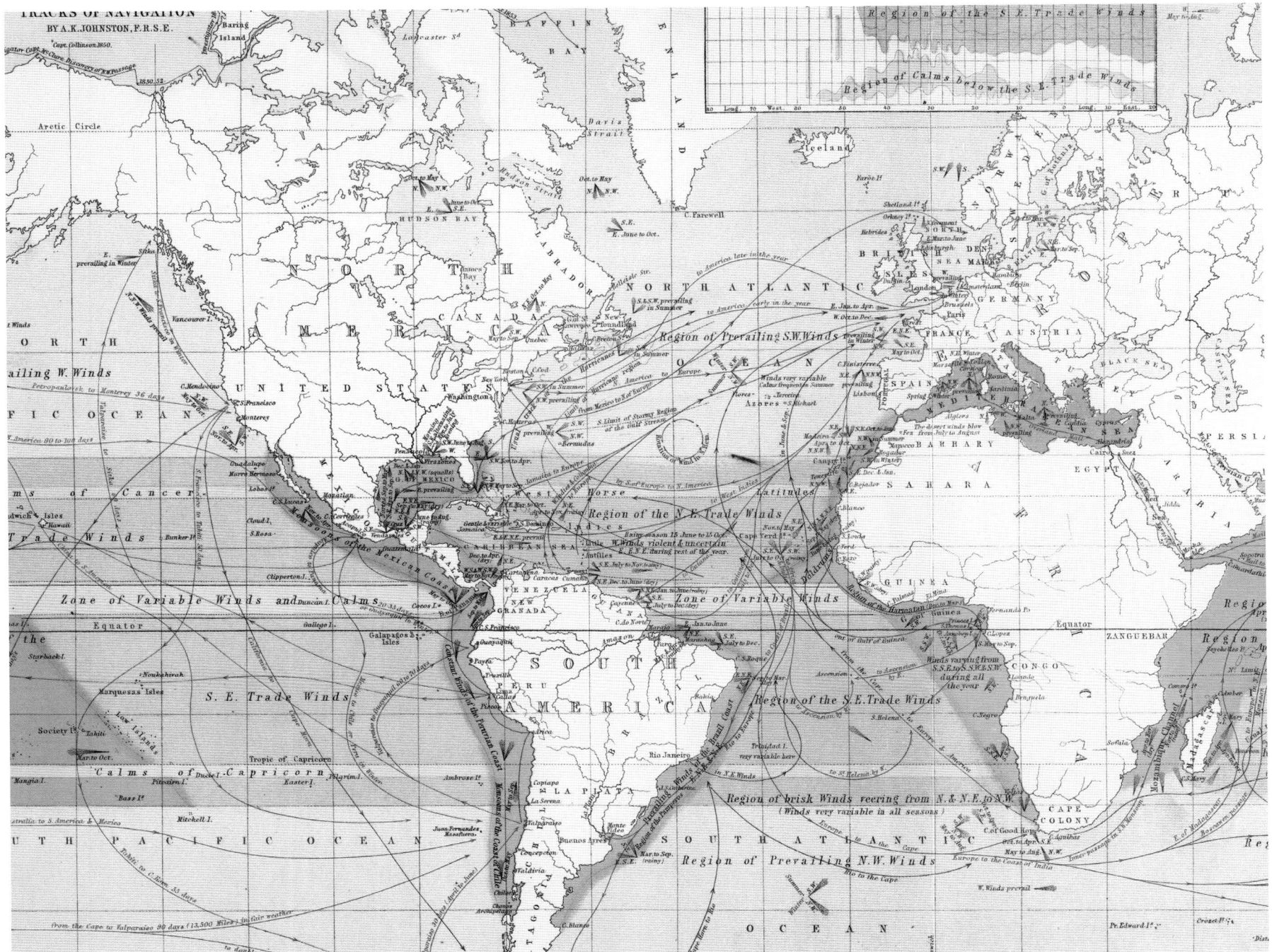
TRACKS OF NAVIGATION
BY A.K. JOHNSTON, F.R.S.E.
Region of the S.E. Trade Winds
Region of Calms below the S.E. Trade Winds
Arctic Circle
Baffin Bay
Davis Strait
Iceland
Hudson Bay
C. Farewell
NORTH ATLANTIC OCEAN
Region of Prevailing S.W. Winds
Region of the N.E. Trade Winds
Zone of Variable Winds and Calms
Zone of Variable Winds
Equator
Calms of Cancer
Calms of Capricorn
Tropic of Capricorn
S.E. Trade Winds
Region of the S.E. Trade Winds
Region of brisk Winds veering from N. & N.E. to N.W.
(Winds very variable in all seasons)
Region of Prevailing N.W. Winds
SOUTH ATLANTIC OCEAN
SOUTH PACIFIC OCEAN
Prevailing W. Winds
UNITED STATES
MEXICO
CANADA
GERMANY
FRANCE
SPAIN
AUSTRIA
EGYPT
SAHARA
GUINEA
CONGO
CAPE COLONY
ZANGUEBAR
Madagascar
Iceland
Azores
Cape Verd Is.
Rio Janeiro
Buenos Ayres
Valparaiso
Lima
Panama
Caracas
Bermudas
Jamaica
Lisbon
Paris
London
Rome
Cairo
Alexandria
Algiers
Malta
Cyprus
Tenerife
Canary Is.
Galapagos Isles
Marquesas Isles
Society Is.
Sandwich Isles
Hawaii
Tahiti
Cape Good Hope
Cape Horn
Pr. Edward Is.
Crozet Is.
Seychelles Is.
Comoro Is.
Mozambique Channel
Sofala
Bass Is.
Mitchell I.
Ambrose Is.
Pitcairn I.
Easter I.
Clipperton I.
Cocos I.
Galapagos Is.
Juan Fernandez
Masafuera
Ascension
St. Helena
Fernando Po
Prince's Is.
St. Thomas I.
Cape Verd Is.
Canary Is.
Madeira
Azores
Faroe Is.
Shetland Is.
Orkney Is.
Hebrides
Malta
Cyprus
Sardinia
Corsica
Sicily
Cairo
Suez
Alexandria
Algiers
Cape Verd Is.
Canary Is.
Madeira
Azores
Lisbon
Paris
London
Rome
Cairo
Alexandria
Algiers
Malta
Cyprus
Tenerife
Canary Is.
Galapagos Is.
Marquesas Is.
Society Is.
Sandwich Is.

Illustration © David Rumsey Map Collection, www.davidrumsey.com

DIE ISOTHERMKURVEN DER NÖRDLICHEN HALBKUGEL

DARGESTELLT IN DER POLAR-PROJECTION

Als weitere Ausführung der im vorigen Blatte gegebenen Darstellung der Isothermen auf der ganzen Erdoberfläche in Merkator's Projection.

Gegründet auf die Untersuchungen von A. v. HUMBOLDT, L. v. Buch, Brewster, Schouw, Kämtz, A. Erman, v. Bær, &c., &c., so wie auf eigene Berechnungen u. Vergleichungen von Berghaus.

Potsdam, 15 Sept. 1837.

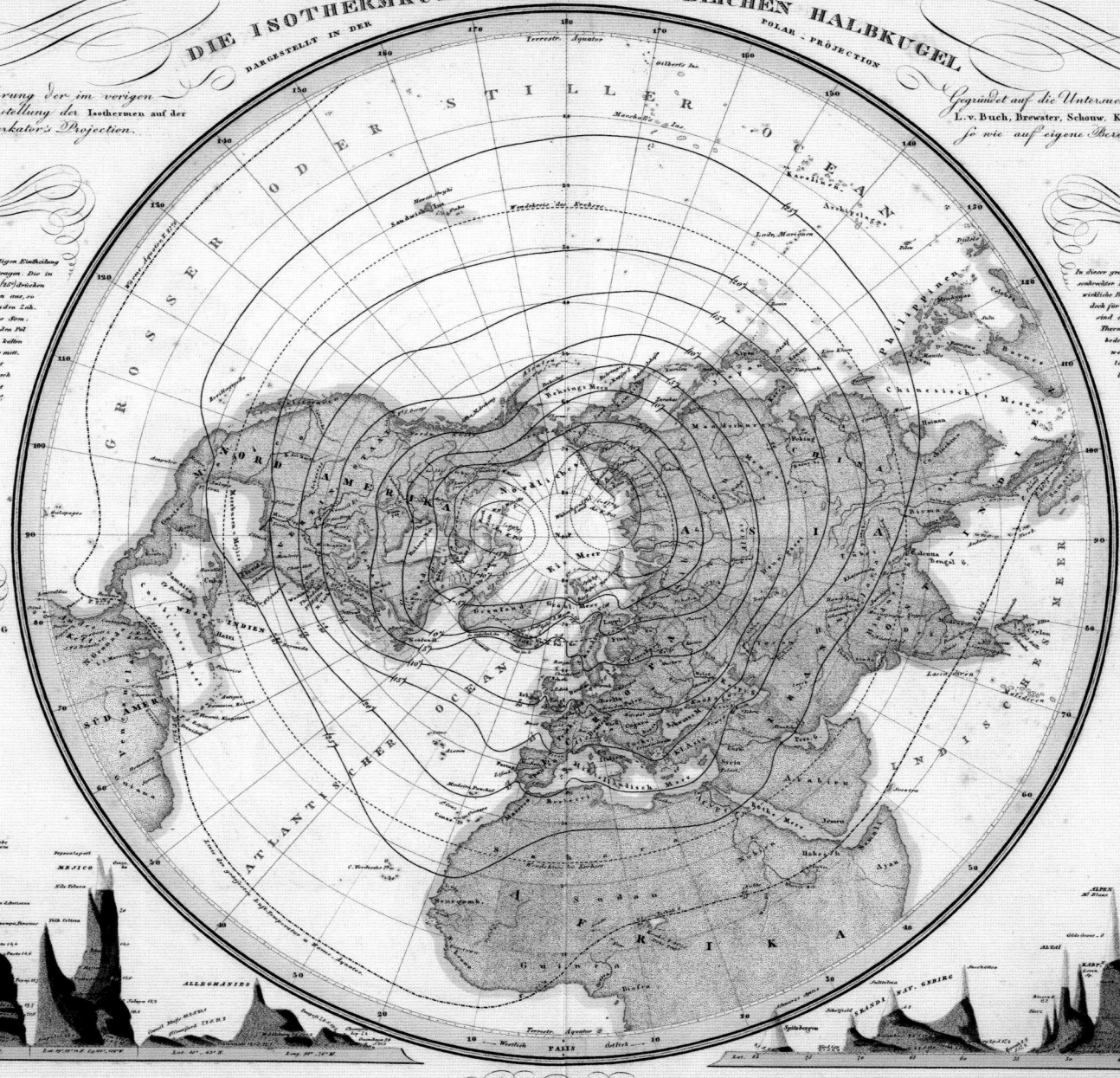

Erläuterungen zur Karte.

Die Isothermen sind nach der hundertheiligen Eintheilung der Thermometer-Skale gerechnet und eingetragen. Die in Parenthese stehenden Temperaturen, z. B. (25°) drücken den Werth einer jeden der Isothermkurven aus, so wie die auf den weitesten davon stehenden Zahlen die Temperaturen des Winters und des Sommers angeben, dergestalt daß die gegen den Pol gerichtete Zahl die mittlere Temperatur des kalten die gegen den Äquator gerichtete Zahl die mittlere Temperatur der warmen Jahreszeit darstellt. Diese Temperaturen sind nach den Meridianen verschieden. So ist z. B. auf der Isothermkurve von 10° im Küstenklima von West-Europa die Temperatur des Winters 2° des Sommers 20°, im Kontinentalklima von Ost-Asien, jene -5° dort 26°, an der Ostküste der Neuen Welt: Temperatur des Winters -1° des Sommers 22°.

Erläuterungen zum Profil.

In dieser graphischen Darstellung von der Abnahme der Wärme in senkrechter Richtung ist, Hinsichts der Schneegränze nur auf wirkliche Beobachtungen Rücksicht genommen worden, die jedoch für Spitzbergen noch etwas unsicher sind. Auch hier sind die Temperaturen nach der Centesimal-Skale des Thermometers gerechnet. Bei diesen Wärme-Angaben bedeutet S. die mittlere Temperatur des Sommers welche auf die Höhe der Schneegränze von wesentlichem Einfluss ist, so hat z. B. Bern ?,?° mittlere Jahrestwärme und 19,9 mittlere Sommer-Wärme. Die mittlere Temperatur der Jahre an der Schneelinie beträgt im Skandinavischen Gebirge, unterm Polarkreis -6,5°; in den Schweizer Alpen -9°; in den Anden von Quito 1?,4, d. h. über Null, denn alle positive Temperaturen sind ohne Zeichen ausgedrückt. Bei der Schneegränze bedeuten N. S., W. O. die Weltgegenden der Gebirgsseiten.

TEMPERATUR IN VERTIK. RICHTUNG NEÜE WELT

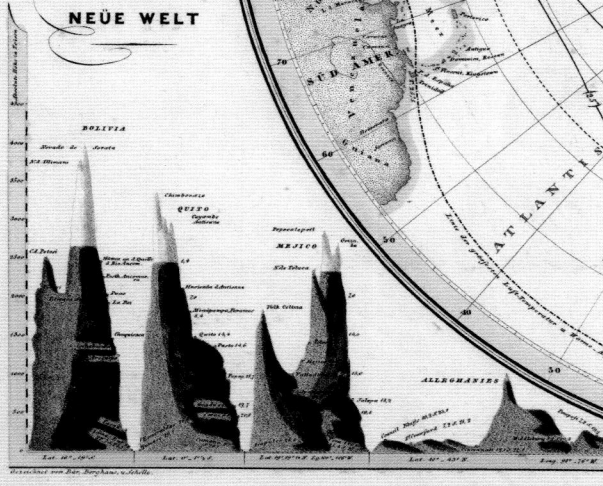

VERHÄLTNISSE UND SCHNEEGRÄNZE ALTE WELT

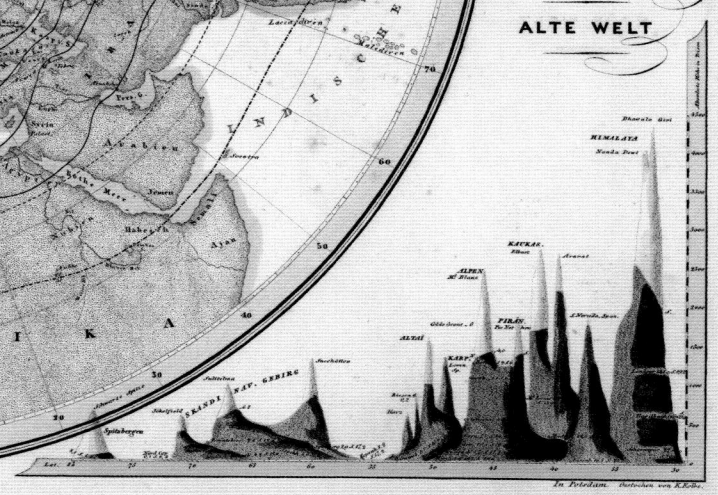

Berichtigt von Bar. Berghaus, u. Schelle.

In Potsdam. Gestochen von K. Keller.

GOTHA J. PERTHES, 1838.

Illustration © David Rumsey Map Collection, www.davidrumsey.com

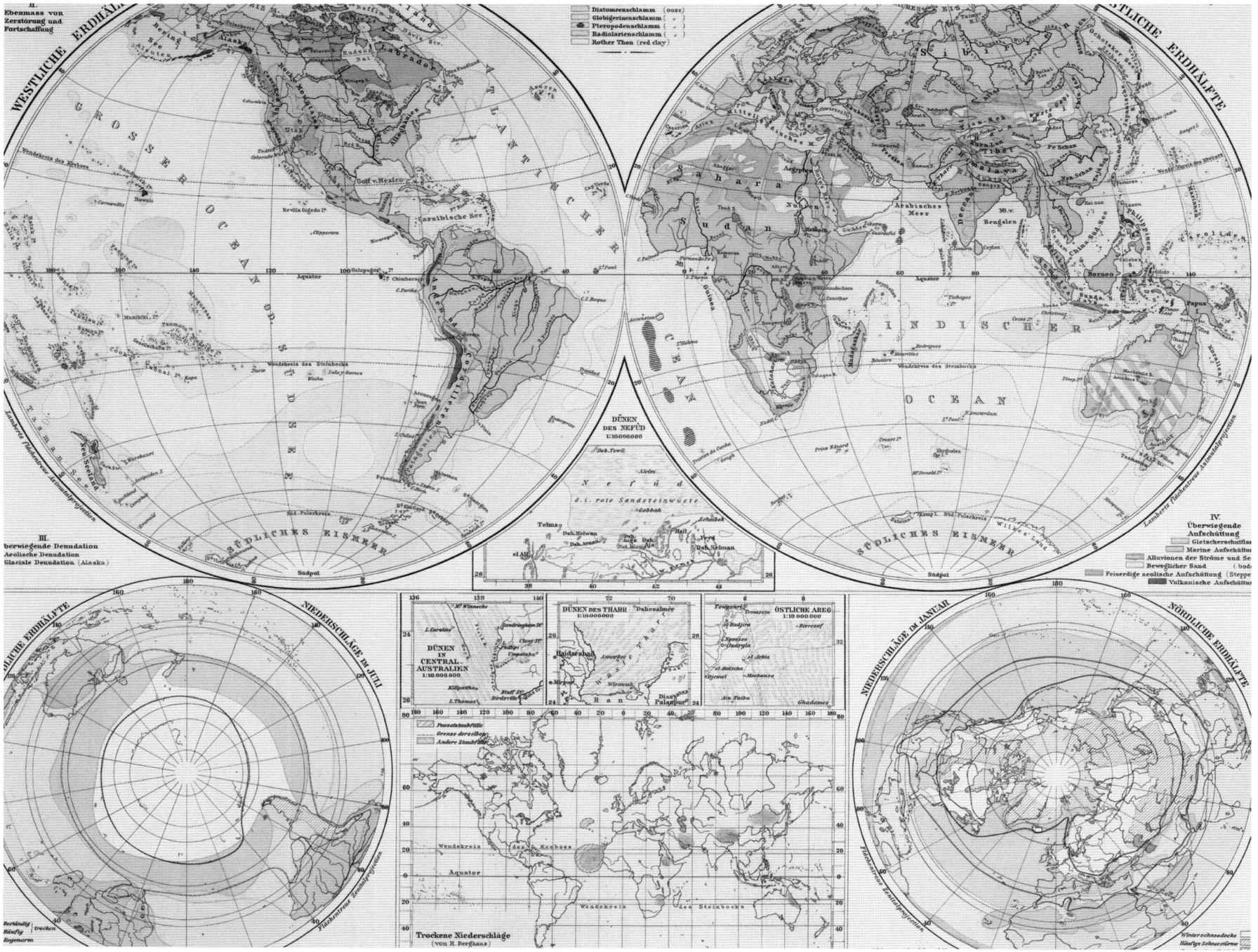
II.
Ebenmass von Zerstörung und Fortschaffung
Diatomeenschlamm (ooze)
Globigerinenschlamm
Pteropodenschlamm
Radiolarienschlamm
Rother Thon (red clay)
WESTLICHE ERDHÄLFTE
ÖSTLICHE ERDHÄLFTE
GROSSER OCEAN
ATLANTISCHER OCEAN
INDISCHER OCEAN
SÜDLICHES EISMEER
Sahara
Sudan
Nubien
Arabisches Meer
Bengalen
Golf v. Mexico
Karibische See
Aequator
Wendekreis des Steinbocks
Südpol
DÜNEN DES NEFÛD
1:10.000.000
Nefûd
d. i. rote Sandsteinwüste
Teima
Hail
Schûbeh
Gobbah
Dsch. Selma
DÜNEN IN CENTRAL AUSTRALIEN
1:10.000.000
DÜNEN DES THARR
1:10.000.000
Thar
Rann
Haidarabad
Palanpur
ÖSTLICHE AREG
1:10.000.000
Ghadames
III.
Überwiegende Denudation
Aeolische Denudation
Glaciale Denudation (Alaska)
IV.
Überwiegende Aufschüttung
Gletscherschuttau
Marine Aufschüttu
Alluvionen der Ströme und Se
Beweglicher Sand (bod
Feinerdige aeolische Aufschüttung (Steppe
Vulkanische Aufschütt
NIEDERSCHLÄGE IM JULI
NIEDERSCHLÄGE IM JANUAR
NÖRDLICHE ERDHÄLFTE
Flächentreue Zenitalprojection
Beständig trocken
Häufig
Regenarm
Wintersschneedecke
Häufige Schneestürme
Trockene Niederschläge
(von H. Berghaus)

Illustration © David Rumsey Map Collection, www.davidrumsey.com

JAHRES-ISOTHERMEN.

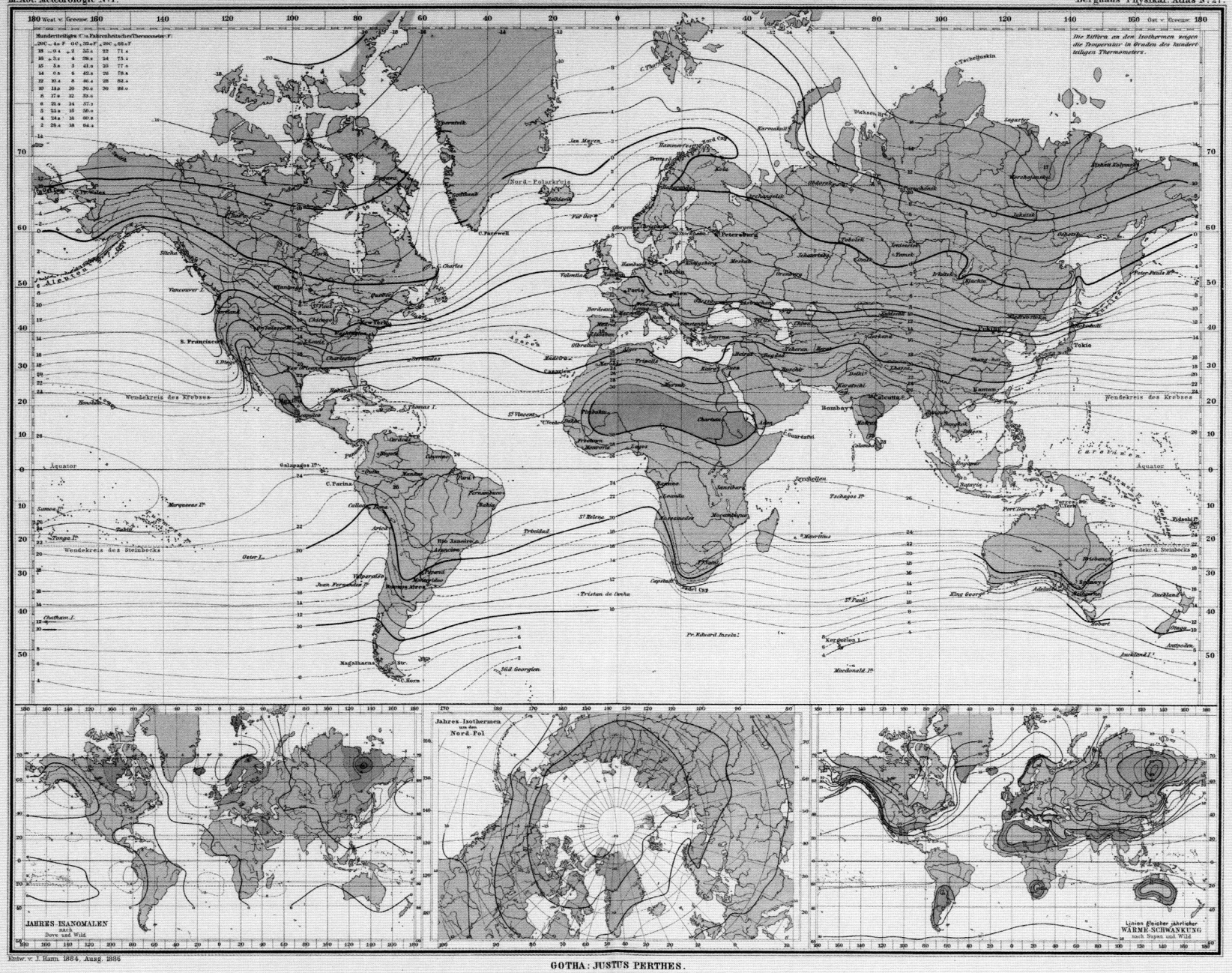

Entw. v. J. Ham. 1884, Ausg. 1886

GOTHA: JUSTUS PERTHES.

Illustration © David Rumsey Map Collection, www.davidrumsey.com

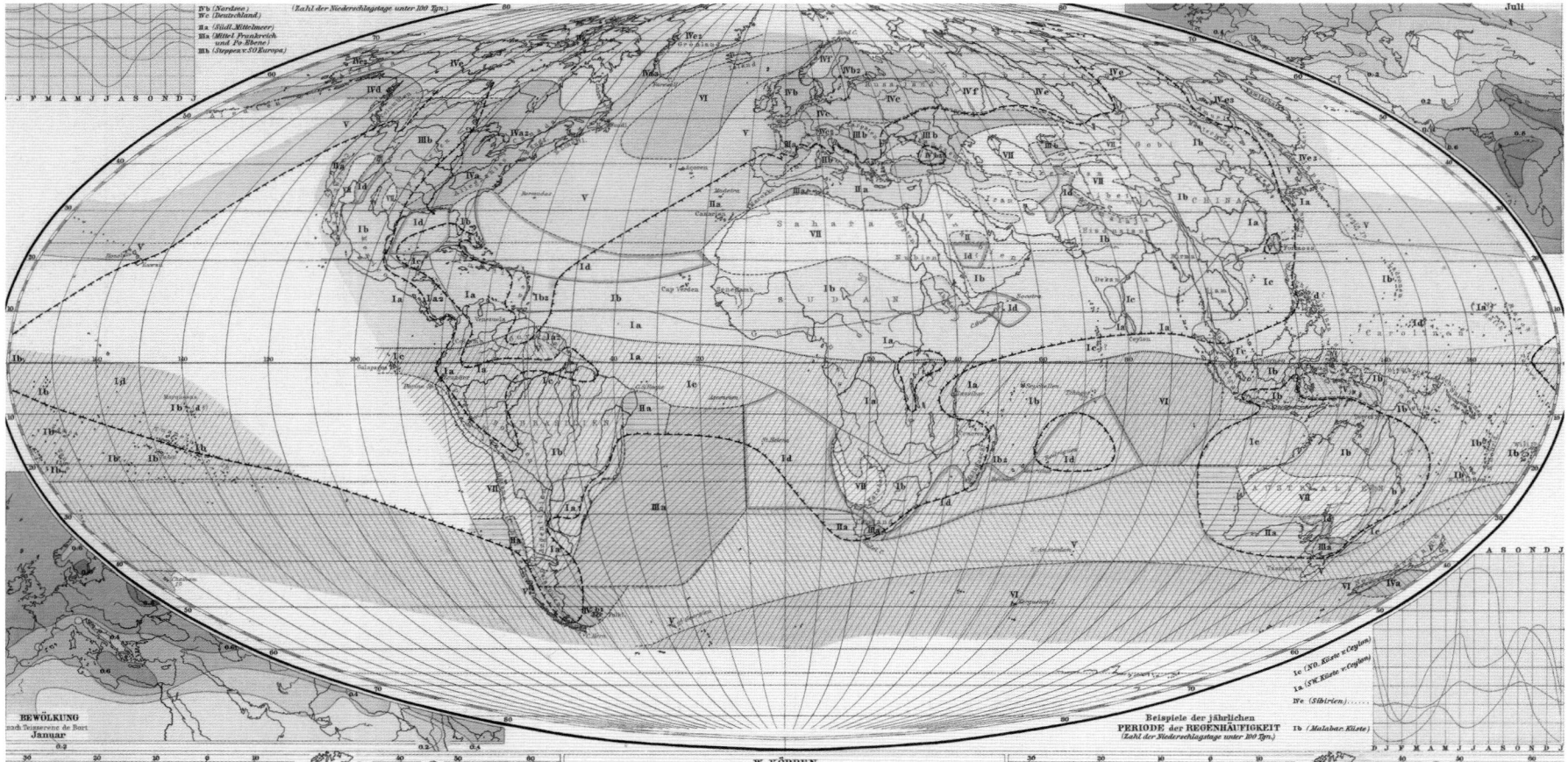
(Zahl der Niederschlagstage unter 100 Tgn.)
IVb (Nordsee)
IVc (Deutschland)
IIa (Südl. Mittelmeer)
IIIa (Mittel Frankreich und Po Ebene)
IIIb (Steppen v. S O Europa)
J F M A M J J A S O N D J
Juli
Sahara
Ceylon
Galapagos
Cap Verden
Madagascar
Kerguelen
Patagonien
Bermuden
Azoren
Madeira
Canaren
Malabar
Sibirien
Mittelmeer

Illustration © David Rumsey Map Collection, www.davidrumsey.com

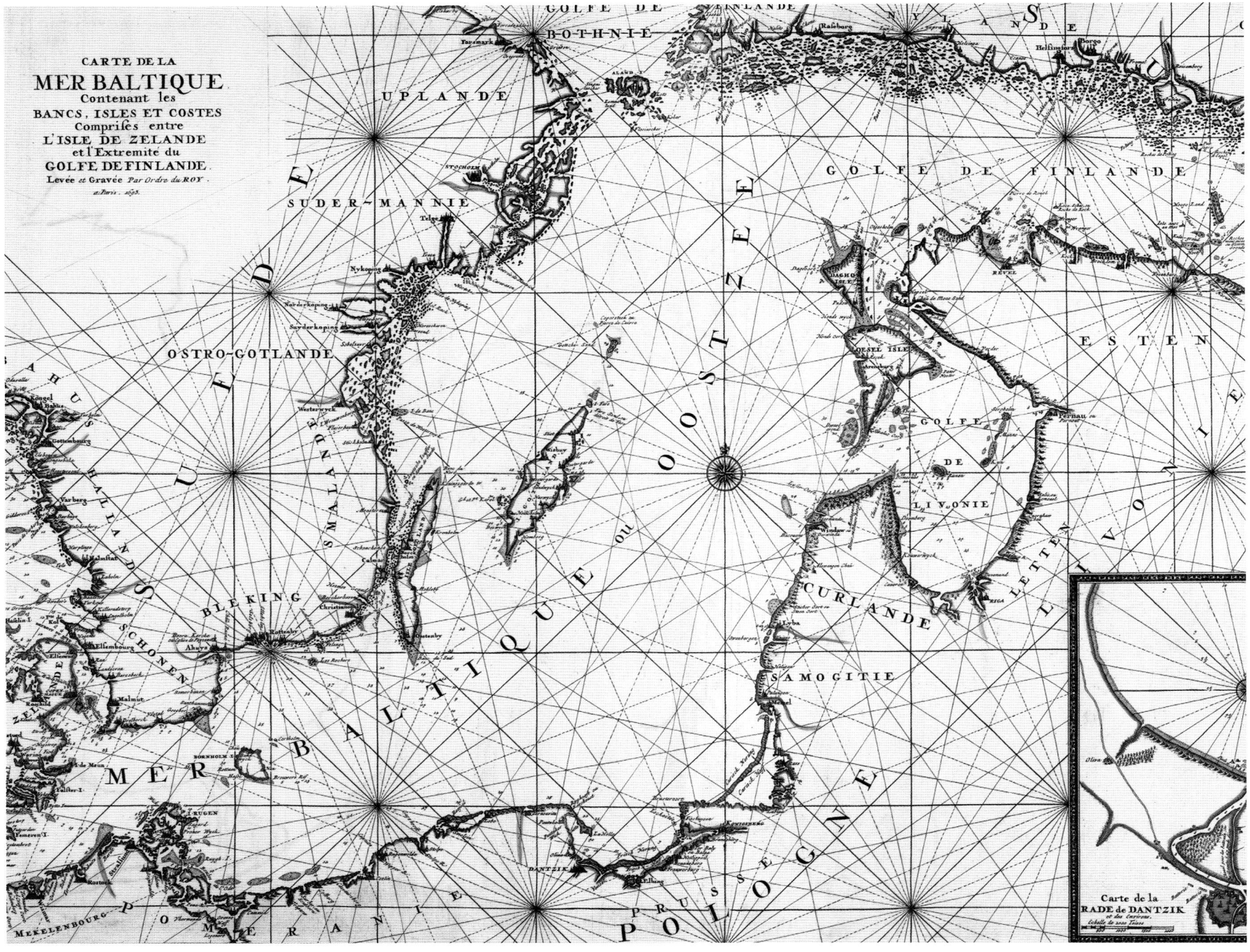
CARTE DE LA
MER BALTIQUE
Contenant les
BANCS, ISLES ET COSTES
Comprises entre
L'ISLE DE ZELANDE
et l'Extremite du
GOLFE DE FINLANDE.
Levée et Gravée Par Ordre du ROY.
a Paris. 1698.
GOLFE DE BOTHNIE
UPLANDE
SUDER-MANNIE
OSTRO-GOTLANDE
GOLFE DE FINLANDE
ESTEN
LIVONIE
CURLANDE
SAMOGITIE
GOLFE DE LIVONIE
MER BALTIQUE ou OOSTZEE
POLOGNE
PRUSSE
POMERANIE
MEKELLENBOURG
SCHONEN
BLEKING
SMALANDE
HALLANDE
ZELANDE
BORNHOLM
ALAND
STOCKHOLM
Telge
Nykoping
Nordekoping
Suyderkoping
Westervyck
Wisby
Calmar
Christianso
Ostesby
Rostoby
Ahuys
Elsenburg
Malmit
Kiel
Varberg
Gottenburg
Kongel
Malstat
Rostock
Stralsund
RUGEN
DANTZIK
Elbing
Konigsberg
Memel
Windau
Pernau
REVEL
RIGA
Helsingfors
Borgo
Raseborg
Carte de la
RADE de DANTZIK
et des environs.
Echelle de 2000 Toises

Illustration © David Rumsey Map Collection, www.davidrumsey.com

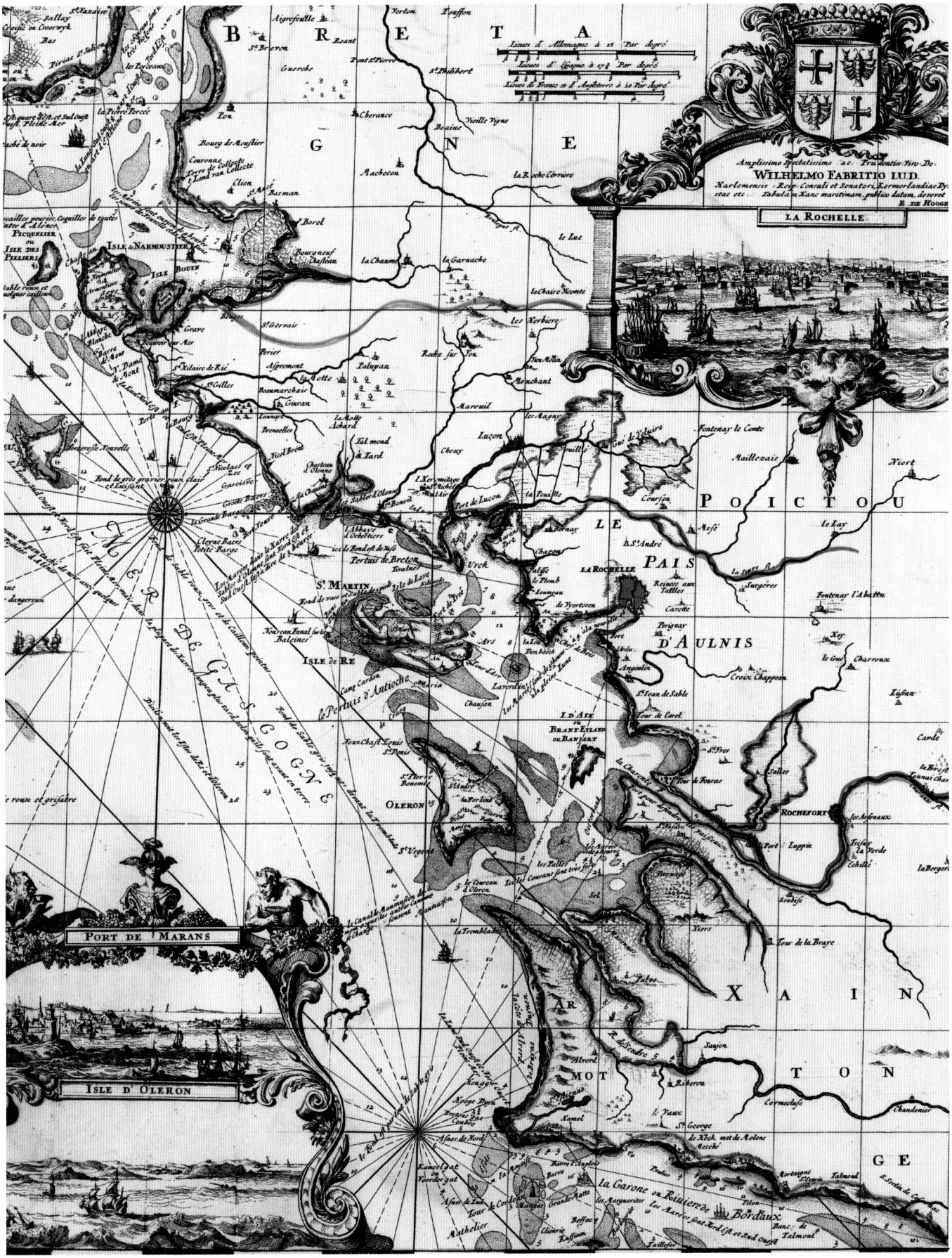
B R E T A G N E
Lieues d'Allemagne à 25 par degré
Lieues d'Espagne à 17½ par degré
Lieues de France et d'Angleterre à 20 par degré
Amplissimo Spectatissimo ac Prudentissimo Viro Do.
WILHELMO FABRITIO IUD.
Harlemensis Reip. Consuli et Senatori, Fermerlandiae Pr
stae etc. Tabulam hanc maritimam publicis datam, devovet
R. DE HOOGE
LA ROCHELLE.
ISLE DE NARMOUSTIER
ISLE BOUIN
PICQUELIER ou ISLE DES PEELIERS
Bourg de Moustier
Bourneuf
Chateau
Machecoin
la Roche Corvoux
Cherance
Vieille Vigne
Beaulieu
Bouin
Borel
Basman
Clion
Couronne
Terre de Collette
Land van Collette
la Chaume
la Garnache
la Chaire Vicomte
le Lac
les Xerbiers
St Gervais
Perier
Aspremont
Talayan
Roche sur Yon
Pen Mille
Monchant
St Gilles
Bournarchais
Guran
Mareuil
Lucon
Les Magnes
Cheux
Fontenay le Comte
Maillezais
Niort
Coursan
POICTOU
LE PAIS D'AULNIS
Port de Lucon
la Pouille
Chacon
Mose
St André
le Lay
Urck
Pertuis de Breton
St Martin
Isle de Re
Ars
Loumpon
de Yvertoron
LA ROCHELLE
Reineis aux Tailles
Surgeres
Fontenay l'Abattu
Carette
Perignay
Xey
Charroux
Le Gue
Croix Chapeau
Angelin
St Jean de Sable
Tour de Corel
Lusan
Candé
Chaume
Chaufan
Laverdin
Le Pertuis d'Antioche
Tour Chast Louis
St Denis
I. D'AIX ou BRANY ÉTLAND ou BANJARS
Tour de Fouras
Salles
ROCHEFORT
les Arsenaux
Fort Luppin
Trisac
la Verde
Echillé
OLERON
St Pierre Bonenne
Stinbre
la Perlond
St Vigeme
les Pallets
Courans sont très forts
Bevenge
Soubise
Sel
Xiers
la Tremblade
Tour de la Brage
Jalot
XAINTONGE
Saujon
Alvert
Rabera
Cormeclase
Chandenier
MOT
St George
Xanel
Asfar de Nord
Asfar de Sud
Tour de Cordouan
Mathelier
Grande Antes
Les Marguerites
Les Marées sont fort forts
la Garone ou Riviere de Bordeaux
Talmond
Taillefer
Bane de Talmond
Port de Marans
Isle d'Oleron

Illustration © David Rumsey Map Collection, www.davidrumsey.com

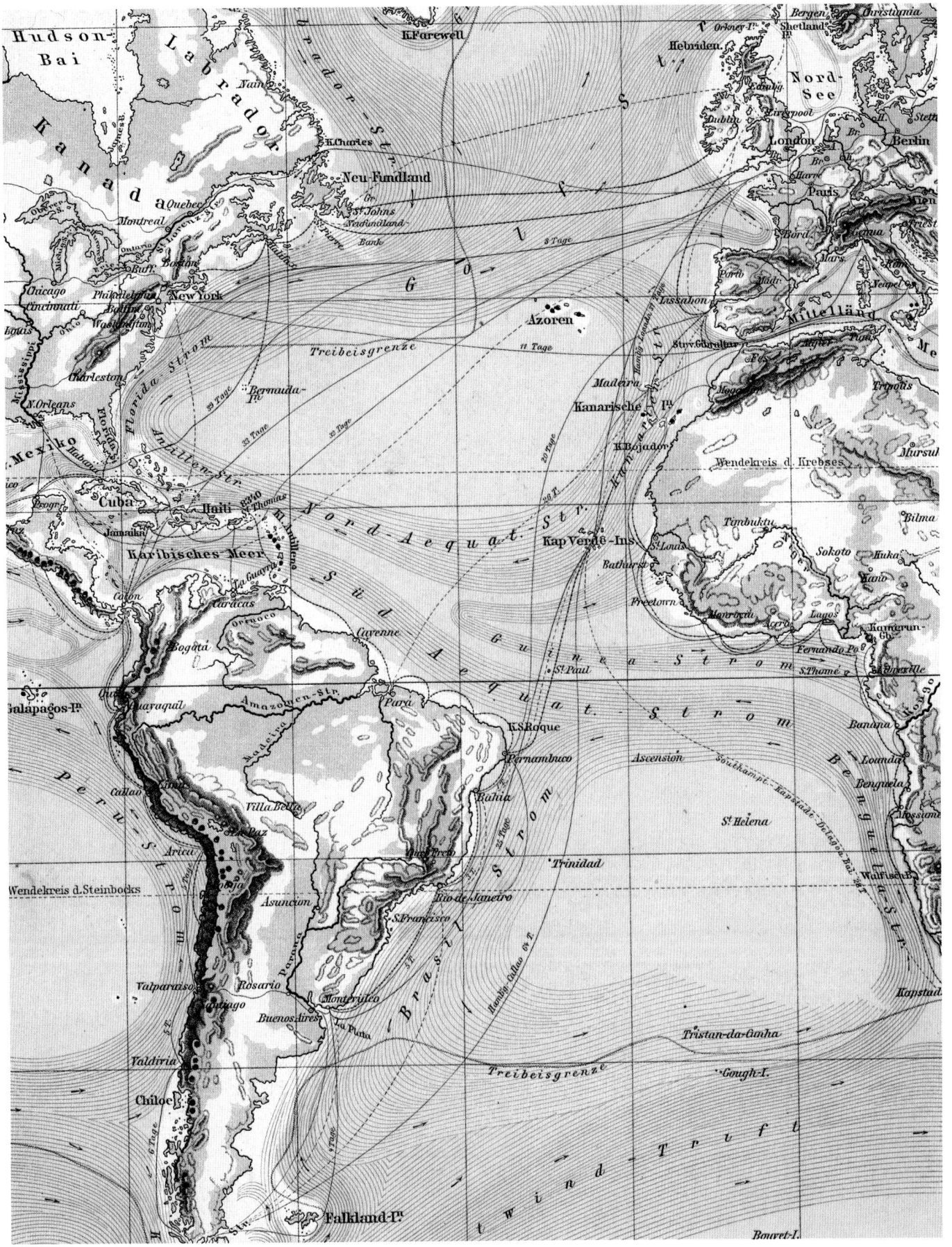
Hudson-Bai
Labrador
Kanada
K. Farewell
Hebriden
Orkney-I.
Bergen
Christiania
Shetland-I.
Nord-See
Nain
K. Charles
Neu-Fundland
St. Johns
Neufundland-Bank
Quebec
Montreal
Boston
New York
Philadelphia
Baltimore
Washington
Chicago
Cincinnati
St. Louis
Charleston
N. Orleans
Florida-Strom
Golf-Strom
Azoren
Lissabon
Madeira
Kanarische I.
K. Bojador
Gibraltar
Madrid
Paris
London
Dublin
Liverpool
Berlin
Wien
Rom
Venedig
Mittelländ. Meer
Tripolis
Mursuk
Wendekreis d. Krebses
Treibeisgrenze
Bermuda-I.
Antillen-Str.
Mexiko
Havana
Cuba
Haiti
St. Thomas
Jamaika
Karibisches Meer
Nord-Aequat.-Str.
Kap Verde-Ins.
St. Louis
Bathurst
Timbuktu
Sokoto
Kuka
Wano
Bilma
Freetown
Monrovia
Accra
Lagos
Kamerun-Gb.
Fernando Po
St. Thomé
Süd-Aequat.-Str.
Guinea-Strom
Caracas
La Guayra
Cayenne
Orinoco
Bogota
Quito
Guayaquil
Galapagos-I.
Amazonen-Str.
Para
St. Paul
K. S. Roque
Pernambuco
Ascension
Southampt. Kapstadt-Dekadenbai
Banana
Loanda
Benguela
Mossamedes
Kongo
Callao
Lima
Peru-Strom
Villa Bella
Bahia
St. Helena
La Paz
Arica
Trinidad
Wendekreis d. Steinbocks
Asuncion
Rio de Janeiro
S. Francisco
Brasil-Strom
Valparaiso
Rosario
Montevideo
Buenos Aires
La Plata
Tristan-da-Cunha
Kapstadt
Valdivia
Chiloe
Gough-I.
Falkland-I.
Bouvet-I.
Passat-Wind-Trift

Illustration © David Rumsey Map Collection, www.davidrumsey.com

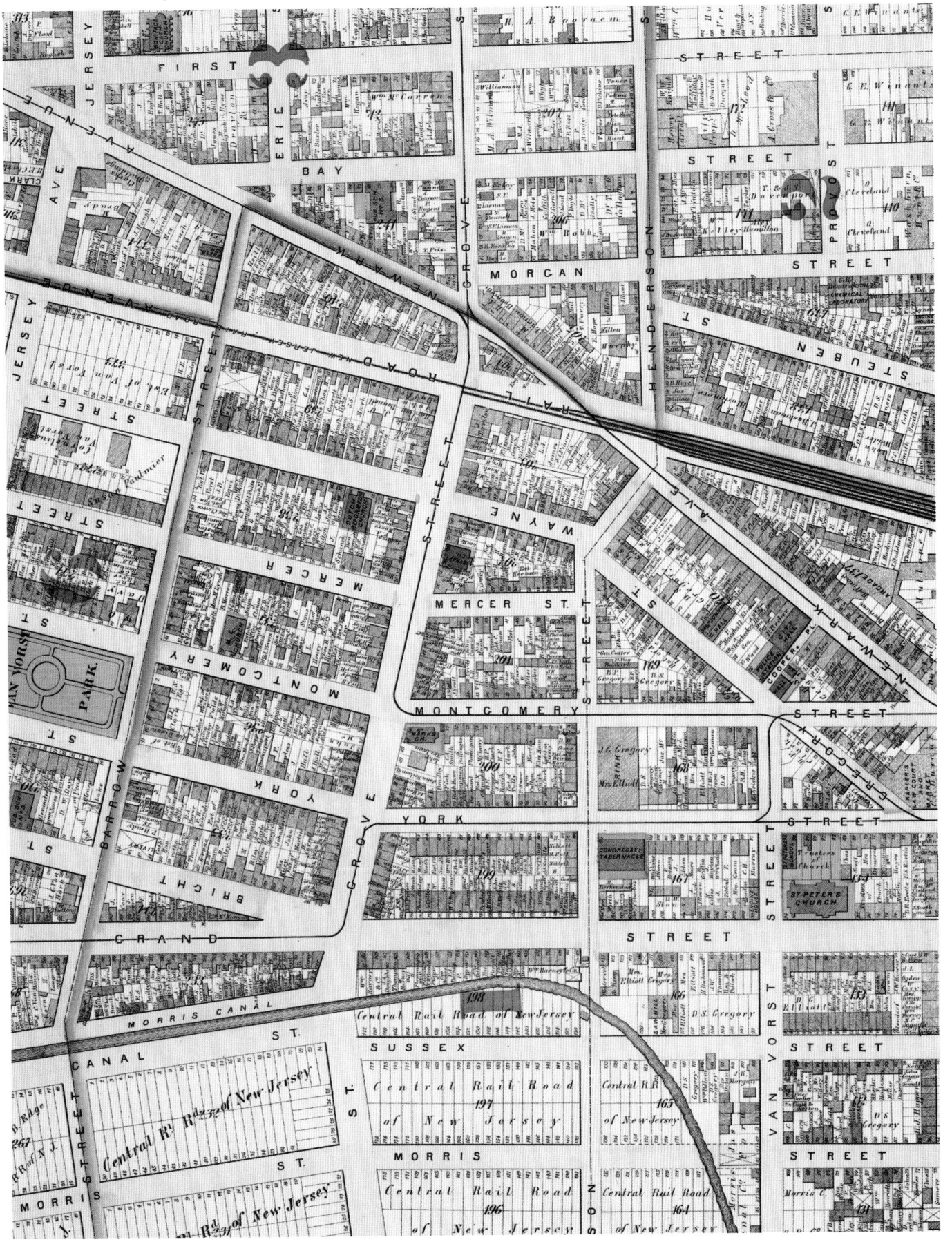
FIRST
STREET
ERIE
BAY
MORCAN
HENDERSON
PROVOST
STREET
STEUBEN
ST
NEWARK
AVENUE
JERSEY
AVE
CLARK
RAILROAD
STREET
WAYNE
MERCER
MERCER ST.
MONTGOMERY
STREET
YORK
STREET
GREGORY
STREET
GROVE
STREET
BARROW
ST
VAN VORST
PARK
BRIGHT
GRAND
MORRIS CANAL
CANAL
ST.
SUSSEX
ST.
MORRIS
ST.
VAN VORST
STREET
Central Rail Road of New Jersey
Central R.R. of New Jersey
Central Rail Road of New Jersey
Central R.R. of New Jersey
Central Rail Road of New Jersey
Central Rail Road of New Jersey
CONGREGATIONAL TABERNACLE
ST PETER'S CHURCH
COOPER PL
D.S. Gregory
Mrs. Elliott
Mrs. Gregory
Mrs. Elliott
Mrs. Gregory
D.S. Gregory
D.S. Gregory
D.S. Gregory
Trustees of Church
Morris C.
198
197
196
199
200
201
168
169
166
167
165
164
133
134
131

Illustration © David Rumsey Map Collection, www.davidrumsey.com

MAP OF THE GEOGRAPHICAL DISTRIBUTION OF THE MOST IMPORTANT PLANTS YIELDING FOOD, INCLUDING THE CULTIVATED GRAINS AND OTHER CULTIVATED AND WILD BREAD PLANTS

WITH INDICATIONS OF THE PRINCIPAL FRUITS: LAID DOWN IN CONNECTION WITH CLIMATAL CONDITIONS FOR KEITH JOHNSTON'S PHYSICAL ATLAS

BY ARTHUR HENFREY, F.R.S. F.L.S. &c.

EXPLANATION.

BARLEY	RYE	OATS	WHEAT	MAIZE	RICE
A	B	C	D	E	F

The Grains are distinguished by reference letters, the colours indicating regio which one or more Grains of a particular kind form the principal objects of corn The names in Black Letters indicate Plants yielding important articles of Foo character analogous to that yielded by Grain (Bread plants) The names in Blue Letters indicate Plants useful in the Arts. The names in Red Letters indicate Characteristic Fruits of the Zones. The narrow Red Lines crossing the Map indicate the lootheres of June, July and A therefore Summer in the N. and Winter in the S. Hemisphere. The narrow Blue lines crossing the Map indicate the lootheres of December, Ja and February, therefore Winter in the N. and Summer in the S. Hemisphere. The broad Blue, and Red Lines indicate Limits or Zones of Vegetation defined by Climate.

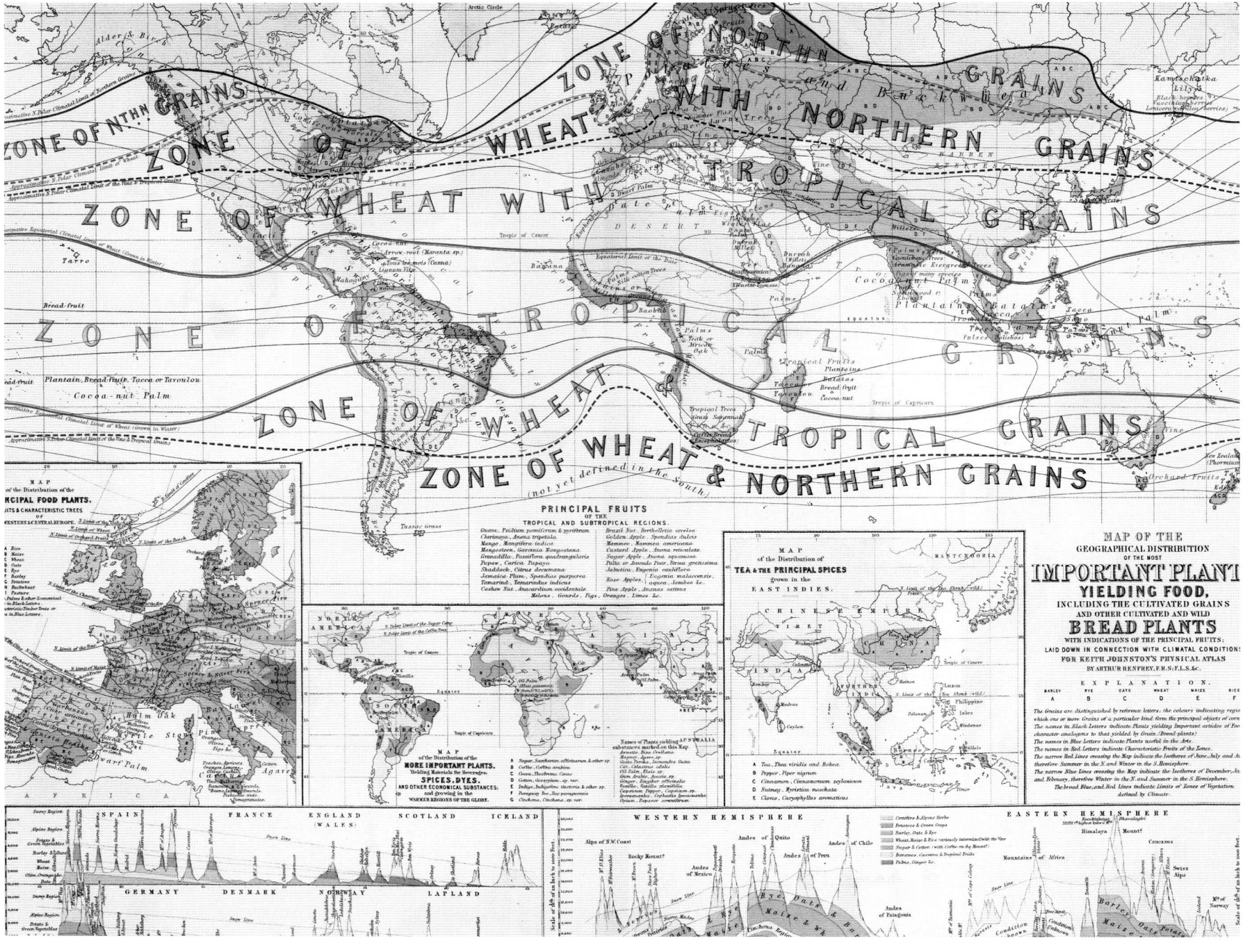
ZONE OF NTHN GRAINS
ZONE OF WHEAT WITH NORTHERN GRAINS
ZONE OF WHEAT WITH TROPICAL GRAINS
ZONE OF TROPICAL GRAINS
ZONE OF WHEAT & TROPICAL GRAINS
ZONE OF WHEAT & NORTHERN GRAINS
(not yet defined in the South)
Arctic Circle
Tropic of Cancer
Tropic of Capricorn
Equator
Bread-fruit
Plantain, Bread-fruit, Tacca or Tavoulou
Cocoa-nut Palm
Tussac Grass
Ramtschatka Lily
Tropical Fruits
Plantains
Bread-fruit
Cocoa-nut
Tropical Trees
Grass Savannah
Tree Bread (Encephalartos)
Orchard Fruits
New Zealand Thormium
Cocoa-nut Palm
Palms
Date palm
Wine Palm
Dwarf Palm
Sago Palm
Oil Palm
Areca Palm
Cocoa-nut Palm
Plantains
Tacca
Sago
Tree Ferns
Tree Fulsies (Balichos)
Tropical Fruits
Plantains
Bread-fruit
Cocoa-nut
Tree Bread (Encephalartos)
Tropical Trees
Grass Savannah
Tree Bread (Encephalartos)
Orchard Fruits
Tree Ferns
Tree Fulsies (Balichos)
Cocoa-nut Palm
Plantains
Tacca
Sago
Tree Ferns
Tree Fulsies (Balichos)
Palms
Teak or Iron-Tree Oak
Bamboos
Palms
Sago
Cocoa-nut
Bread-fruit
Tacca
Tavoulou

Illustration © David Rumsey Map Collection, www.davidrumsey.com

GEOGRAPHICAL DISTRIBUTION
OF
INDIGENOUS VEGETATION.

The Distribution of Plants in a perpendicular direction
IN THE TORRID, TEMPERATE AND FRIGID ZONES,
with indications of the Mean Temperature of the Year and of the coldest and warmest months.

BY A.K. JOHNSTON, F.R.S.E. & ARTHUR BENFREY, F.R.S. E.L.S. &c.

ANDES

TORRID ZONE, LAT. 0°–10°
(Humboldt, Bonpland, Pentland.)

TENERIFFE

LAT. 27½–28½°
(Buch, Smith)

HIMALAYA

TEMPERATE — LAT. 29°–32° — ZONE
(Hooker, Thompson, Jacquemont, Royle &c.)

ALPS & PYRENEES

LAT. 42°–46° N.
(Wahlenberg, Buch, Schouw, Ramond, De Candolle)

LAPLAND

FRIGID ZONE LAT. 68°
(Buch, Wahlenberg)

(Spain)

EQUATORIAL	TROPICAL	SUB-TROPICAL	WARM TEMPERATE	COLD TEMPERATE	SUB-ARCTIC	ARCTIC
	19° N.L.	28° N.L.	37° N.L.	46°47° N.L.	62° N.L.	69° N.L.

Snow Line; Alpine Herbs; Alpine Shrubs; Conifers &c.; Deciduous Forest Trees; Evergreen Trees; Laurels & Myrtles; Palms & Bananas; Tree Ferns and Figs; Laurels and Myrtles; Evergreen Trees; Deciduous Forest Trees; Conifers and Birches; Alpine Shrubs

NOTE
Mean temperature expressed th
Temperature of the coldest month
warmest
Names of places be not botanical are engraved in

NOPSIS
of the
RAPHICAL REGIONS
ding to Schouw.

(Explored by)

1	Wahlenberg
2	Linnæus
3	De Candolle
4	Michaux
5	Pursh
6	Kämpfer
7	Roxburgh
8	Wallich
9	Blumenbach
10	Blume
11	Chamisso
12	Forskal
13	Delile
14	Adanson
15	Jacquin
16	Bonpland
17	Humboldt
18	Ruiz & Pavon
19	Schwartz
20	Martius
21	St Hilaire
22	D'Urville
23	Thunberg
24	Brown
25	Forster

S OF PLANTS

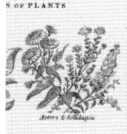

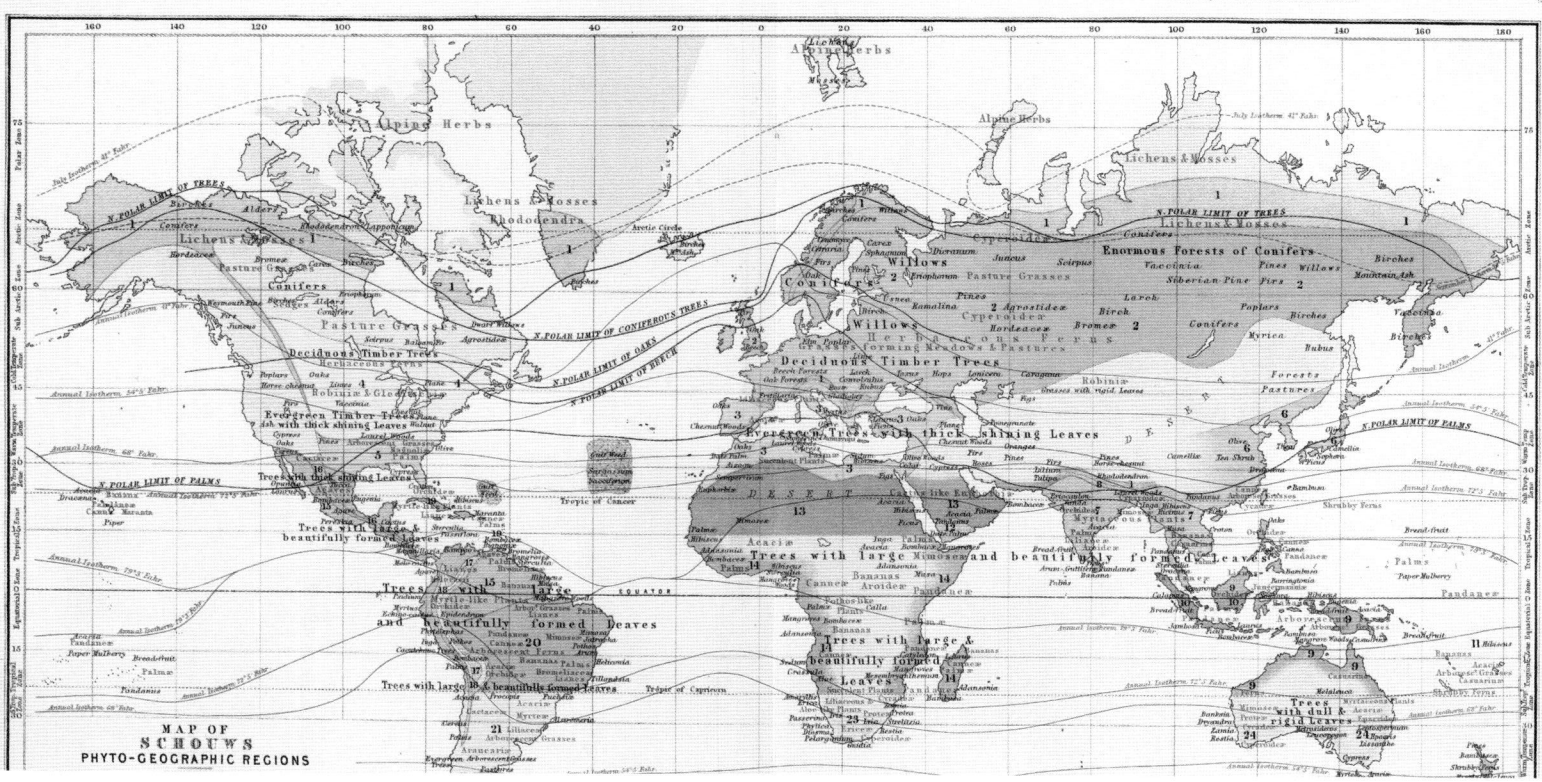

GRAPHICAL S
of the most im
FAMILIES OF
The scale expresses the precen

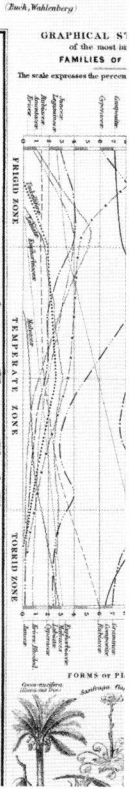

Illustration © David Rumsey Map Collection, www.davidrumsey.com

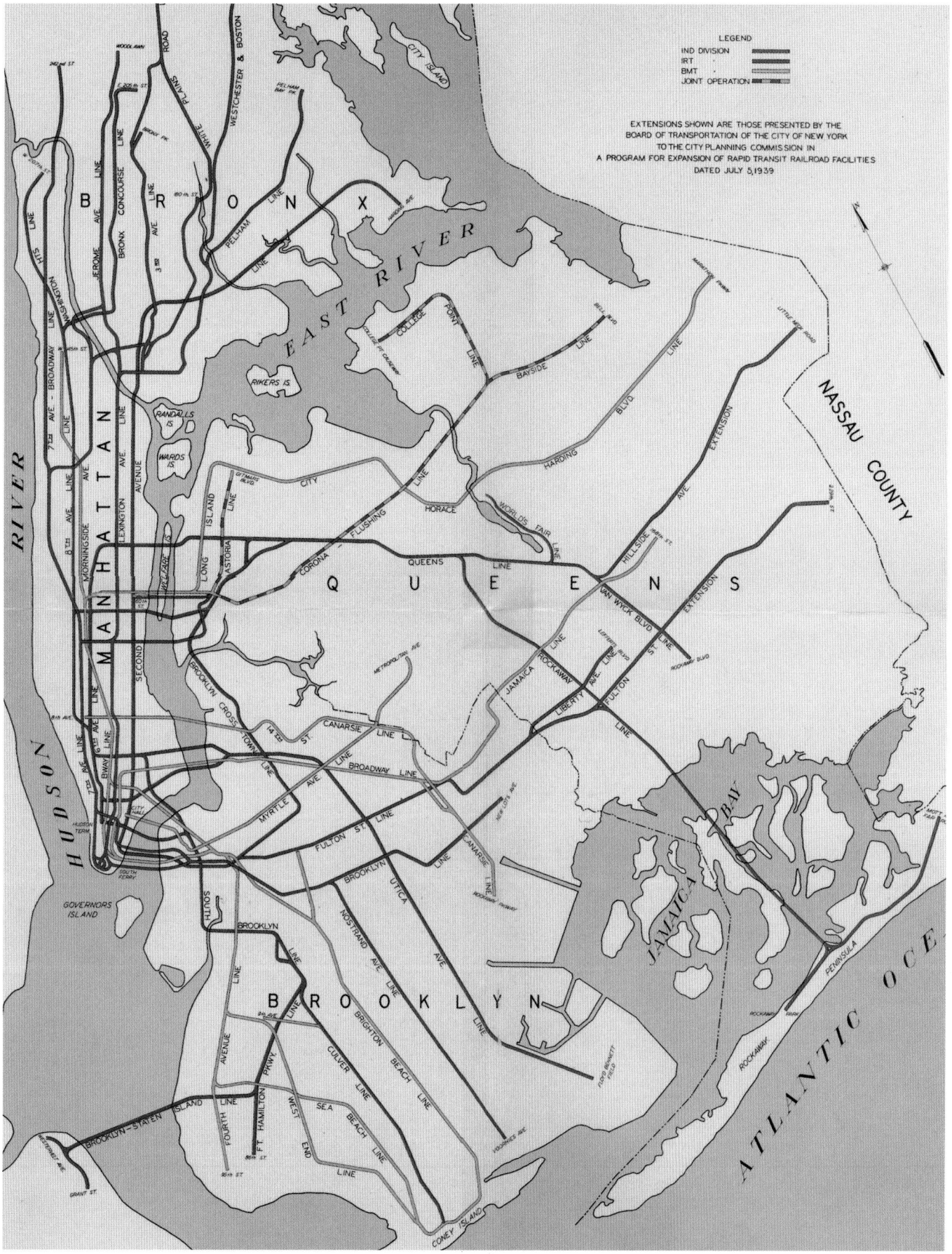
LEGEND
IND DIVISION
IRT
BMT
JOINT OPERATION
EXTENSIONS SHOWN ARE THOSE PRESENTED BY THE
BOARD OF TRANSPORTATION OF THE CITY OF NEW YORK
TO THE CITY PLANNING COMMISSION IN
A PROGRAM FOR EXPANSION OF RAPID TRANSIT RAILROAD FACILITIES
DATED JULY 5, 1939
BRONX
EAST RIVER
MANHATTAN
QUEENS
BROOKLYN
NASSAU COUNTY
HUDSON RIVER
JAMAICA BAY
ATLANTIC OCEAN
CITY ISLAND
RIKERS IS.
RANDALLS IS.
WARDS IS.
GOVERNORS ISLAND
WESTCHESTER & BOSTON
PELHAM LINE
WHITE PLAINS ROAD
3RD AVE LINE
BRONX CONCOURSE LINE
JEROME AVE LINE
LEXINGTON AVE LINE
7TH AVE - BROADWAY LINE
8TH AVE LINE
MORNINGSIDE AVE LINE
SECOND AVENUE
BMT LINE
CITY HALL
SOUTH FERRY
HUDSON TERM
BROOKLYN CROSS TOWN LINE
LONG ISLAND CITY
ASTORIA LINE
CORONA
FLUSHING LINE
COLLEGE POINT LINE
BAYSIDE LINE
HORACE HARDING BLVD
WORLD'S FAIR LINE
HILLSIDE AVE EXTENSION
VAN WYCK BLVD
JAMAICA ROCKAWAY LINE
LIBERTY AVE LINE
FULTON ST LINE
CANARSIE LINE
14TH ST
BROADWAY LINE
MYRTLE AVE
FULTON ST LINE
BROOKLYN UTICA AVE
NOSTRAND AVE LINE
SOUTH BROOKLYN LINE
BRIGHTON BEACH LINE
CULVER LINE
SEA BEACH LINE
WEST END LINE
FOURTH AVENUE LINE
FT HAMILTON PKWY
BROOKLYN-STATEN ISLAND
CONEY ISLAND
PENINSULA
ROCKAWAY

Illustration © Commons.Wikimedia.org/wiki/File:1939_IND_Second_System.jpg

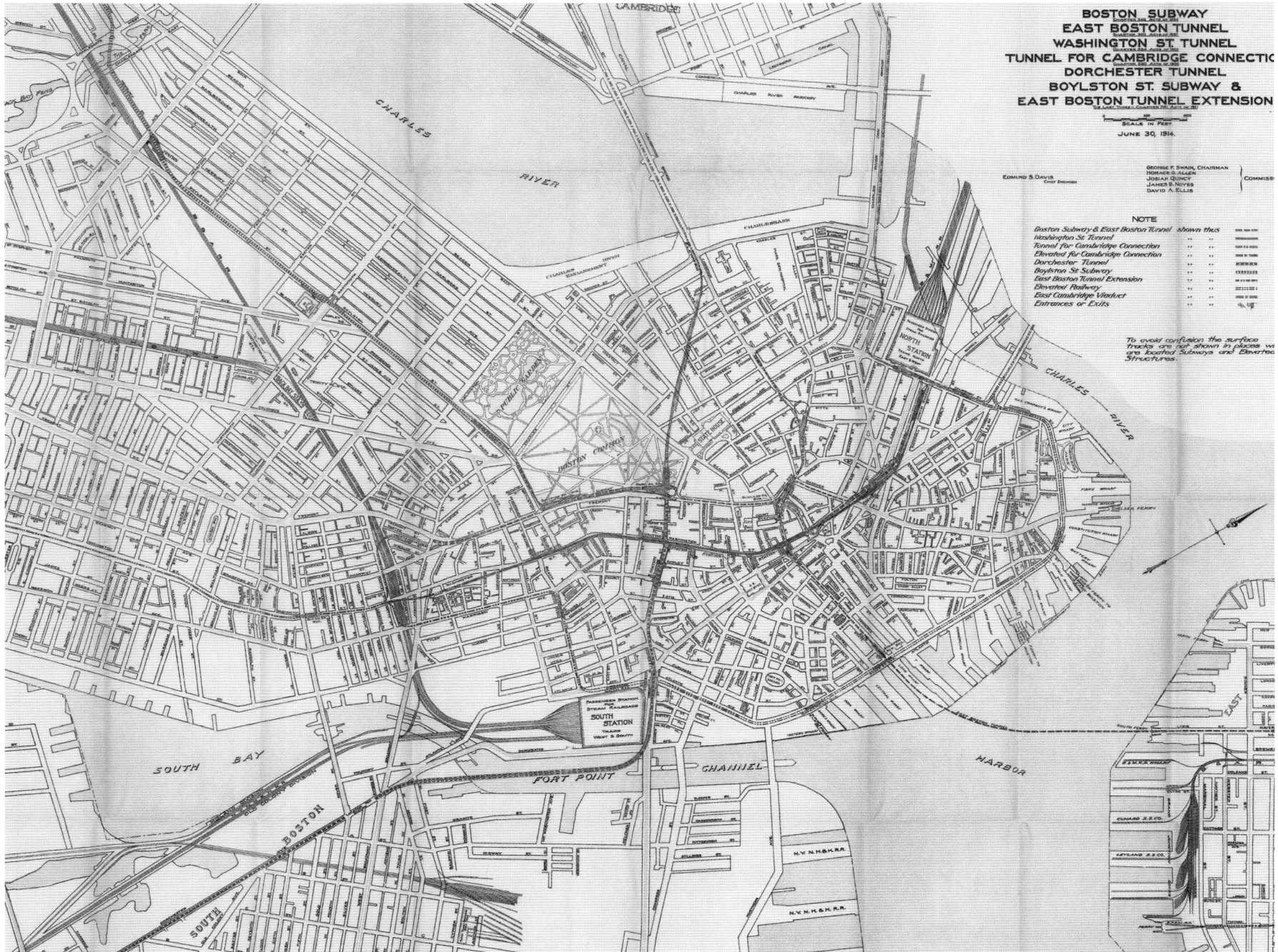
BOSTON SUBWAY
EAST BOSTON TUNNEL
WASHINGTON ST. TUNNEL
TUNNEL FOR CAMBRIDGE CONNECTIO
DORCHESTER TUNNEL
BOYLSTON ST. SUBWAY &
EAST BOSTON TUNNEL EXTENSION
SCALE IN FEET
JUNE 30, 1914.
EDMUND S. DAVIS
CHIEF ENGINEER
GEORGE F. SWAIN, CHAIRMAN
HORACE G. ALLEN
JOSIAH QUINCY
JAMES B. NOYES
DAVID A. ELLIS
COMMISSI
NOTE
Boston Subway & East Boston Tunnel shown thus
Washington St. Tunnel
Tunnel for Cambridge Connection
Elevated for Cambridge Connection
Dorchester Tunnel
Boylston St. Subway
East Boston Tunnel Extension
Elevated Railway
East Cambridge Viaduct
Entrances or Exits
To avoid confusion the surface tracks are not shown in places where are located Subways and Elevated Structures.
CAMBRIDGE
CHARLES
RIVER
CHARLES RIVER
CHARLESBANK
PUBLIC GARDEN
BOSTON COMMON
NORTH STATION
SOUTH STATION
SOUTH BAY
BOSTON
SOUTH
FORT POINT
CHANNEL
HARBOR
EAST
N.Y. N.H. & H.R.R.
CUNARD S.S.CO.
LEYLAND S.S.CO.

Illustration © Commons.Wikimedia.org/wiki/File:1914_BTC_subway_map.png

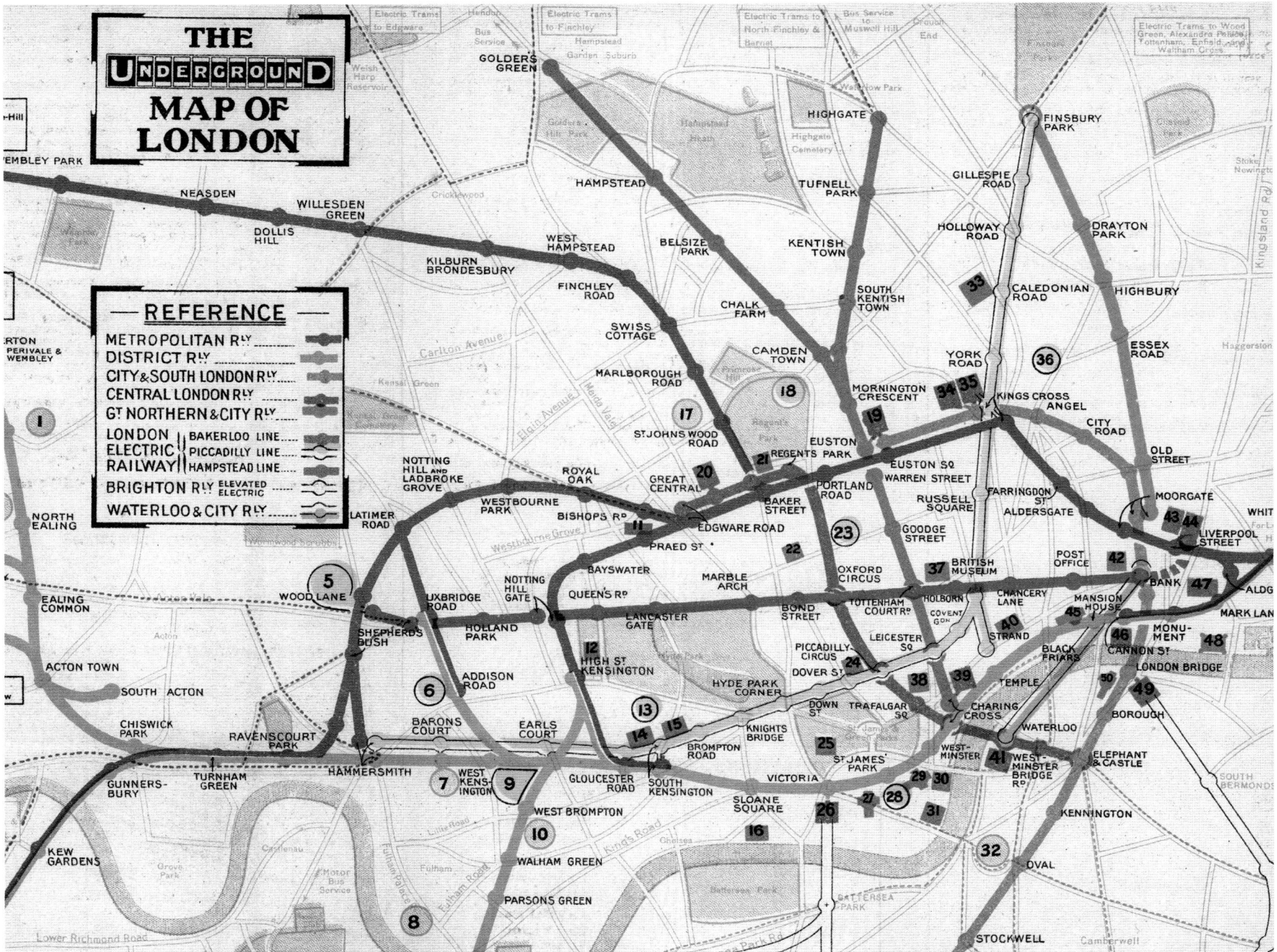
THE UNDERGROUND MAP OF LONDON
REFERENCE
METROPOLITAN RLY
DISTRICT RLY
CITY & SOUTH LONDON RLY
CENTRAL LONDON RLY
GT NORTHERN & CITY RLY
LONDON ELECTRIC RAILWAY
BAKERLOO LINE
PICCADILLY LINE
HAMPSTEAD LINE
BRIGHTON RLY ELEVATED ELECTRIC
WATERLOO & CITY RLY
GOLDERS GREEN
HIGHGATE
FINSBURY PARK
WEMBLEY PARK
NEASDEN
WILLESDEN GREEN
DOLLIS HILL
HAMPSTEAD
TUFNELL PARK
GILLESPIE ROAD
KILBURN BRONDESBURY
WEST HAMPSTEAD
BELSIZE PARK
KENTISH TOWN
HOLLOWAY ROAD
DRAYTON PARK
FINCHLEY ROAD
CHALK FARM
SOUTH KENTISH TOWN
CALEDONIAN ROAD
HIGHBURY
SWISS COTTAGE
CAMDEN TOWN
YORK ROAD
ESSEX ROAD
MARLBOROUGH ROAD
MORNINGTON CRESCENT
KINGS CROSS
ANGEL
CITY ROAD
ST JOHNS WOOD ROAD
EUSTON
REGENTS PARK
EUSTON SQ
OLD STREET
NOTTING HILL AND LADBROKE GROVE
ROYAL OAK
GREAT CENTRAL
WARREN STREET
PORTLAND ROAD
RUSSELL SQUARE
FARRINGDON ST
MOORGATE
NORTH EALING
LATIMER ROAD
WESTBOURNE PARK
BISHOPS RD
BAKER STREET
ALDERSGATE
EDGWARE ROAD
GOODGE STREET
LIVERPOOL STREET
PRAED ST
POST OFFICE
BAYSWATER
MARBLE ARCH
OXFORD CIRCUS
BRITISH MUSEUM
BANK
WOOD LANE
NOTTING HILL GATE
UXBRIDGE ROAD
QUEEN'S RD
TOTTENHAM COURT RD
HOLBORN
CHANCERY LANE
MANSION HOUSE
EALING COMMON
LANCASTER GATE
BOND STREET
COVENT GDN
SHEPHERDS BUSH
HOLLAND PARK
LEICESTER SQ
STRAND
MONUMENT
CANNON ST
PICCADILLY CIRCUS
BLACK FRIARS
ACTON TOWN
HIGH ST KENSINGTON
DOVER ST
LONDON BRIDGE
SOUTH ACTON
ADDISON ROAD
HYDE PARK CORNER
TEMPLE
DOWN ST
TRAFALGAR SQ
CHARING CROSS
CHISWICK PARK
BARONS COURT
EARLS COURT
KNIGHTS BRIDGE
WATERLOO
BOROUGH
RAVENSCOURT PARK
BROMPTON ROAD
ST JAMES' PARK
WEST-MINSTER
WEST-MINSTER BRIDGE RD
ELEPHANT & CASTLE
GUNNERS-BURY
TURNHAM GREEN
HAMMERSMITH
WEST KENS-INGTON
GLOUCESTER ROAD
SOUTH KENSINGTON
VICTORIA
SLOANE SQUARE
WEST BROMPTON
KENNINGTON
KEW GARDENS
WALHAM GREEN
OVAL
PARSONS GREEN
STOCKWELL
CLAPHAM

Illustration © David Rumsey Map Collection, www.davidrumsey.com

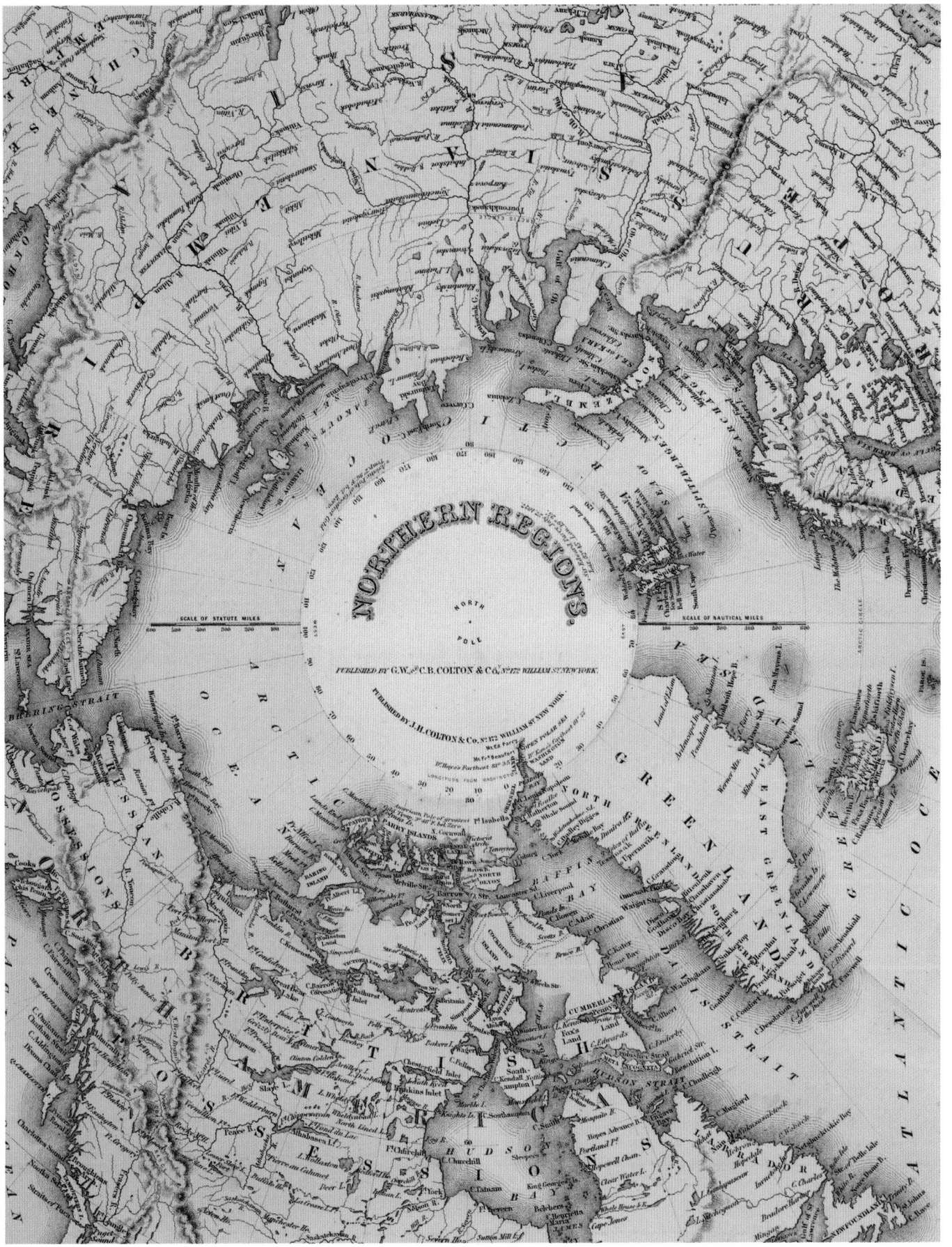
NORTHERN REGIONS.
NORTH POLE
PUBLISHED BY G.W. & C.B. COLTON & CO. Nos 172 WILLIAM ST NEW YORK.
PUBLISHED BY J.H. COLTON & Co. Nos 172 WILLIAM ST NEW YORK.
SCALE OF STATUTE MILES
SCALE OF NAUTICAL MILES
LONGITUDE FROM WASHINGTON
BERING STRAIT
ARCTIC OCEAN
GREENLAND
BAFFIN BAY
HUDSON BAY
HUDSON STRAIT
NORTH WEST PASSAGE
FARRY ISLANDS
BARING ISLAND
CUMBERLAND PEninsula
Fox's Land
Foxe Channel
Iceberg Sta.
Cape Jones
Sutton Mill

Illustration © David Rumsey Map Collection, www.davidrumsey.com

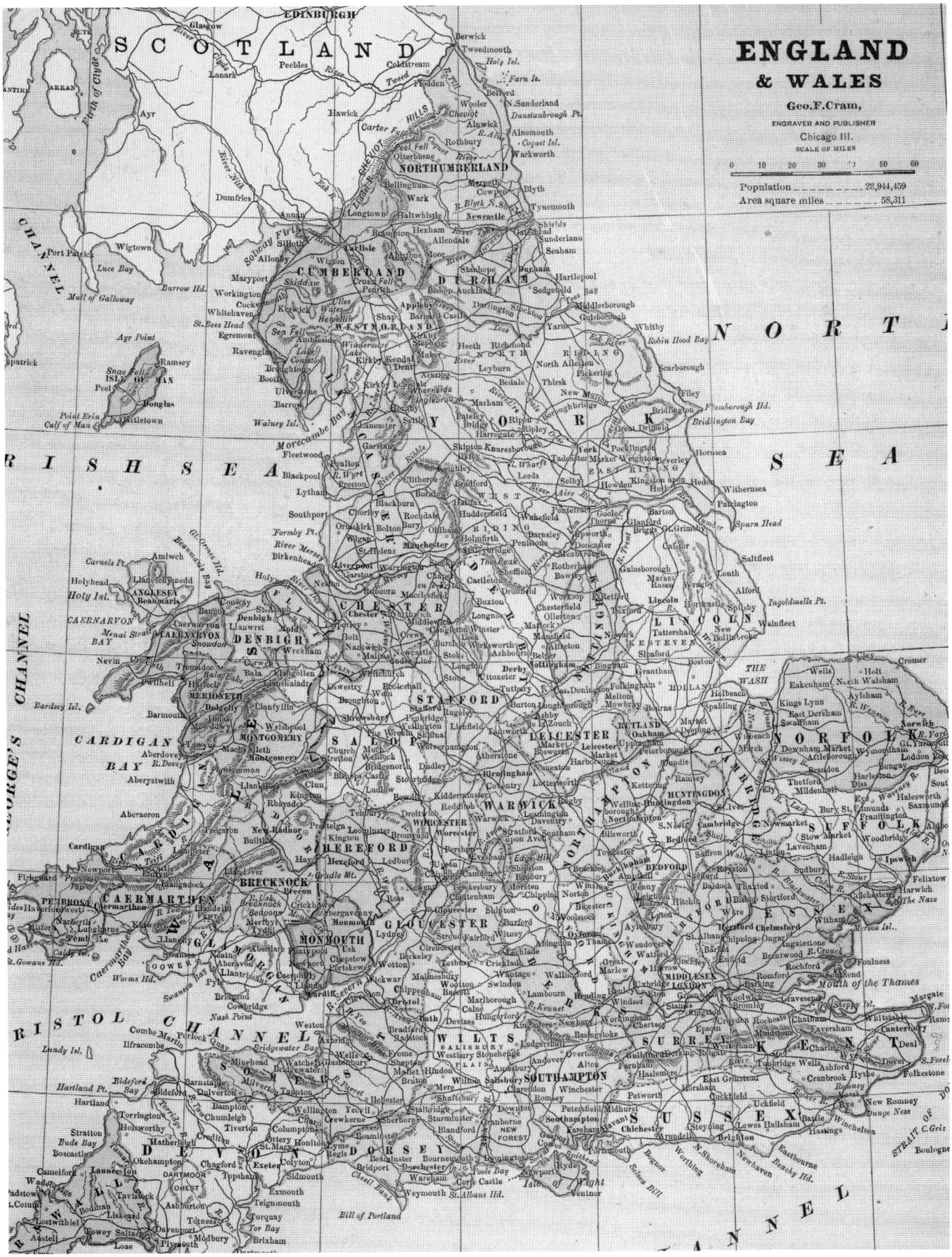
ENGLAND
& WALES
Geo.F.Cram,
ENGRAVER AND PUBLISHER
Chicago Ill.
SCALE OF MILES
0 10 20 30 40 50 60
Population 23,944,459
Area square miles 58,311
SCOTLAND
EDINBURGH
Glasgow
Firth of Clyde
Arran
Ayr
Dumfries
Annan
Carlisle
Wigtown
Port Patrick
Luce Bay
Mull of Galloway
Burrow Hd.
Solway Firth
Silloth
Allonby
Maryport
Workington
Cockermouth
Whitehaven
St. Bees Head
Egremont
Ravenglass
Ayr Point
Ramsey
Peel
ISLE OF MAN
Douglas
Castletown
Point Erin
Calf of Man
Walney Isl.
Morecambe Bay
Fleetwood
Blackpool
Lytham
Southport
Formby Pt.
Amlwch
Carnels Pt.
Holyhead
Holy Isl.
ANGLESEY
Beaumaris
CAERNARVON BAY
Menai Strait
CAERNARVON
Snowdon
Nevin
Pwllheli
Bardsey Isl.
Barmouth
MERIONETH
Dolgelly
Bangor
Conway
Denbigh
Llanwrst
Mold
DENBIGH
Wrexham
Corwen
Bala
Llangollen
Llanrhaiadr
Holywell
Chester
Northwich
Nantwich
Malpas
Whitchurch
Oswestry
Wem
Shrewsbury
Welshpool
MONTGOMERY
Machynlleth
Montgomery
Llanidloes
Aberystwith
Aberaeron
Tregaron
Cardigan
Lampeter
Newcastle Emlyn
Llandovery
Llangadock
Newport
Fishguard
Haverfordwest
PEMBROKE
Carmarthen
CARMARTHEN
Llandeilo
Llandilo
Llanelly
Swansea
Neath
Aberavon
Llantrisant
Pyle
Bridgend
Cowbridge
Caerphilly
Cardiff
Newport
Chepstow
Monmouth
MONMOUTH
Usk
Pontypool
Abergavenny
Merthyr Tydfil
Brecknock
BRECKNOCK
Brecon
Hereford
HEREFORD
Ledbury
Leominster
Kington
Presteign
New Radnor
Builth
Bromyard
Worcester
WORCESTER
Droitwich
Tenbury
Bewdley
Kidderminster
Stourbridge
Dudley
Wolverhampton
Lichfield
Tamworth
Birmingham
Coventry
Warwick
WARWICK
Leamington
Stratford upon Avon
Southam
Banbury
Shipston
Moreton
Chipping Norton
Woodstock
Oxford
Abingdon
Thame
Aylesbury
Tewkesbury
Cheltenham
Gloucester
GLOUCESTER
Stroud
Fairford
Witney
Burford
Cirencester
Tetbury
Cricklade
Lechlade
Malmesbury
Wotton
Chippenham
Bristol
Bath
Devizes
Marlborough
Swindon
Wantage
Wallingford
Abingdon
Henley
Reading
Windsor
Staines
Kingston
Croydon
Epsom
Guildford
Farnham
Haslemere
Dorking
Reigate
Tonbridge
Tunbridge Wells
Ashford
Hythe
Folkestone
Dover
Deal
Canterbury
Margate
Ramsgate
Whitstable
Faversham
Maidstone
Rochester
Chatham
Gravesend
Southend
Rochford
Chelmsford
Colchester
Harwich
Felixstowe
Ipswich
Woodbridge
Stowmarket
Bury St. Edmunds
Newmarket
Cambridge
Ely
Thetford
Mildenhall
Lavenham
Hadleigh
Sudbury
Saffron Walden
Royston
Baldock
Hitchin
Hertford
Ware
Bishop Stortford
Leighton Buzzard
Aylesbury
Tring
Watford
St. Albans
Barnet
Enfield
Hertford
Ongar
Brentwood
Romford
Barking
Rochford
Southend
Mouth of the Thames
Gravesend
Rochester
Chatham
Maidstone
Canterbury
Whitstable
Margate
Ramsgate
Deal
Dover
Folkestone
Hythe
Romney
New Romney
Dungeness
Rye
Winchelsea
Hastings
Battle
Lewes
Hailsham
Eastbourne
Beachy Hd.
Newhaven
Brighton
Shoreham
Worthing
Arundel
Chichester
Bognor
Selsey Bill
Portsmouth
Gosport
Southampton
Winchester
Alton
Andover
Salisbury
Amesbury
Stonehenge
Westbury
Frome
Shepton Mallet
Wells
Glastonbury
Bridgewater
Taunton
Ilminster
Chard
Axminster
Honiton
Exeter
Topsham
Sidmouth
Exmouth
Teignmouth
Torquay
Tor Bay
Brixham
Dartmouth
Totnes
Modbury
Plymouth
Saltash
Fowey
Lostwithiel
Bodmin
Liskeard
Launceston
Tavistock
Okehampton
Chagford
Ashburton
Crediton
Tiverton
Barnstaple
Ilfracombe
Bideford
Hartland
Torrington
Holsworthy
Stratton
Bude Bay
Boscastle
Camelford
Wadebridge
Padstow
St. Colum
St. Ives
Lundy Isl.
Hartland Pt.
Bideford Bay
Barnstaple Bay
Bristol Channel
Nash Point
Worms Hd.
Caldy Isl.
St. Gowans Hd.
Cardigan Bay
Aberystwith
Bardsey Isl.
Holy Isl.
Menai Strait
Beaumaris Bay
Gt. Ormes Hd.
Formby Pt.
Bill of Portland
Chesil Bank
Weymouth
St. Albans Hd.
Poole Bay
Isle of Wight
Ventnor
Cowes
Spithead
Portsmouth
Selsey Bill
Bognor
Worthing
N. Shoreham
Newhaven
Beachy Hd.
Eastbourne
Hastings
Winchelsea
Dungeness
Folkestone
Boulogne
STRAIT OF C. Gris
Dover
Margate
Ramsgate
Whitstable
Canterbury
Deal
Mouth of the Thames
Southend
Rochford
Colchester
Harwich
Felixstowe
Ipswich
Woodbridge
Saxmundham
Aldeburgh
Yarmouth
Gt. Yarmouth
Norwich
Wymondham
Loddon
Bungay
Beccles
Halesworth
Eye
Diss
Harleston
Thetford
Brandon
Downham Market
Swaffham
Fakenham
Wells
Holt
North Walsham
Aylsham
Cromer
Cley
Lynn
Kings Lynn
East Dereham
Swaffham
Wisbeach
March
Ely
Newmarket
Bury St. Edmunds
Stowmarket
Woodbridge
Ipswich
Felixstowe
Harwich
Colchester
Southend
Rochford
Romford
Barking
Brentwood
Ongar
Chelmsford

Illustration © David Rumsey Map Collection, www.davidrumsey.com

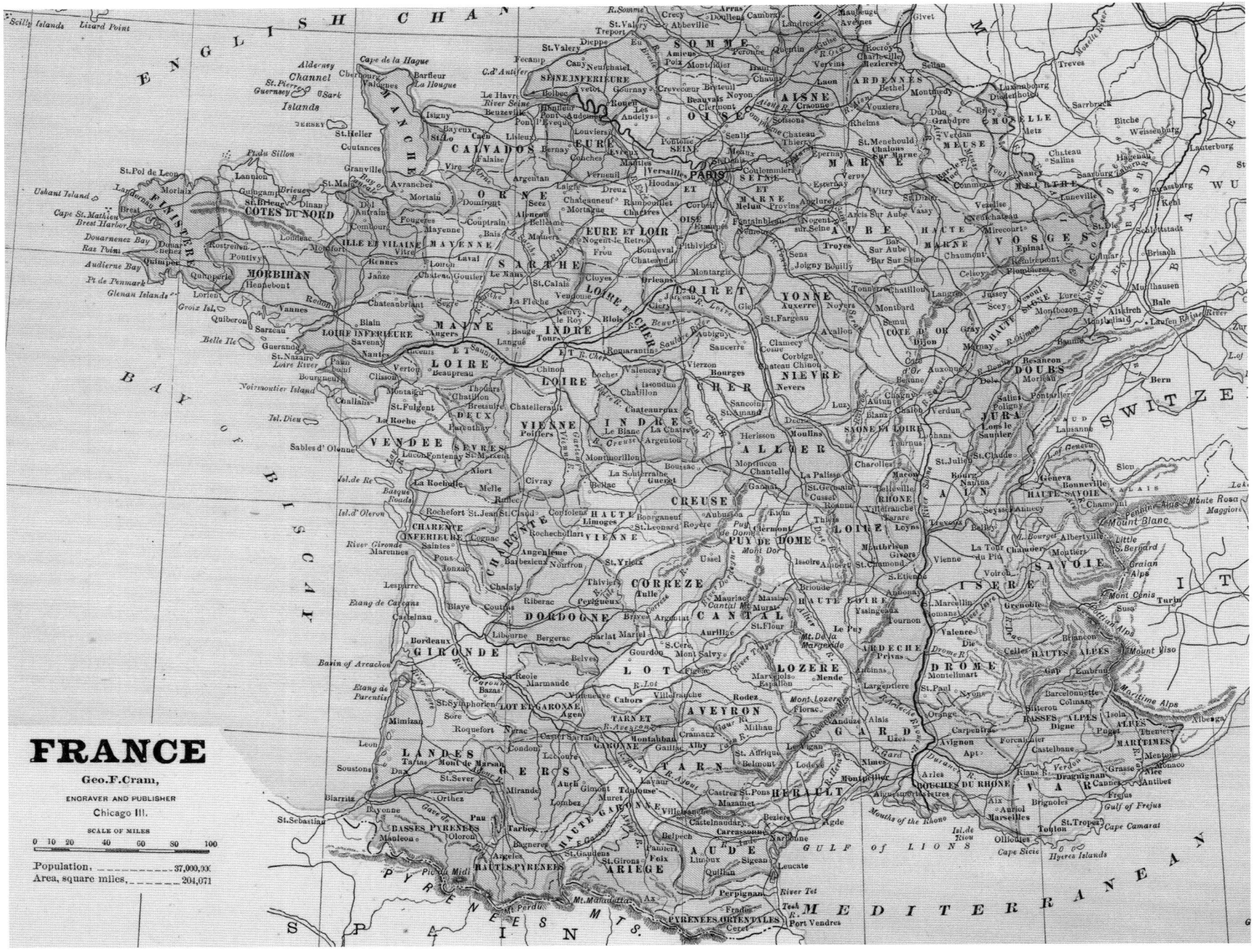
FRANCE
Geo.F.Cram,
ENGRAVER AND PUBLISHER
Chicago Ill.
SCALE OF MILES
0 10 20 40 60 80 100
Population, 37,000,000
Area, square miles, 204,071
ENGLISH CHANNEL
BAY OF BISCAY
MEDITERRANEAN
GULF of LIONS
SWITZERLAND
SPAIN
PARIS
SEINE
SEINE INFERIEURE
SOMME
OISE
AISNE
ARDENNES
MOSELLE
MEUSE
MARNE
MEURTHE
VOSGES
AUBE
HAUTE MARNE
YONNE
COTE D'OR
DOUBS
JURA
NIEVRE
SAONE ET LOIRE
AIN
HAUTE SAVOIE
SAVOIE
ISERE
RHONE
LOIRE
PUY DE DOME
ALLIER
CHER
INDRE
CREUSE
HAUTE VIENNE
VIENNE
CORREZE
CANTAL
HAUTE LOIRE
ARDECHE
DROME
HAUTES ALPES
BASSES ALPES
ALPES MARITIMES
VAR
BOUCHES DU RHONE
GARD
LOZERE
HERAULT
AUDE
PYRENEES ORIENTALES
AVEYRON
TARN
TARN ET GARONNE
LOT
LOT ET GARONNE
DORDOGNE
GIRONDE
LANDES
GERS
HAUTE GARONNE
HAUTES PYRENEES
BASSES PYRENEES
ARIEGE
LOIRE INFERIEURE
MAINE ET LOIRE
SARTHE
MAYENNE
ORNE
EURE
EURE ET LOIR
LOIRE ET CHER
CALVADOS
MANCHE
ILLE ET VILAINE
COTES DU NORD
FINISTERE
MORBIHAN
VENDEE
DEUX SEVRES
CHARENTE
CHARENTE INFERIEURE
JERSEY
Channel Islands
Aldernay
Guernsey
Sark
St. Pierre
Cape de la Hague
Cape St. Mathieu
Brest Harbor
Douarnenez Bay
Raz Toini
Audierne Bay
Pt de Penmark
Glenan Islands
Belle Ile
Noirmoutier Island
Isl. Dieu
Isl. de Re
Isl. d'Oleron
Basque Roads
Basin of Arcachon
Etang de Parentis
Etang de Caseans
River Gironde
Pic du Midi
Mt. Perdu
Mt. Maladetta
Mouths of the Rhone
Isl. de Riou
Cape Sicie
Hyeres Islands
Gulf of Frejus
Cape Camarat
Mont Cenis
Mount Viso
Mont Blanc
Monte Rosa
Maggiore
Maritime Alps
Cottian Alps
Graian Alps
Little S. Bernard
Mt. Lozere
Mt. Dore
Puy de Dome
Cantal Mts
Mt. de la Margeride
Mt. Cenis
Mt. Mandelotta
Pic du Midi
Mt. Perdu
River Tet
Tech R.
Port Vendres
Perpignan
Ceret
Frades
Prades
Mt. Cenis
Mt. Mandelotta
Mt. Perdu
Pic du Midi

Illustration © David Rumsey Map Collection, www.davidrumsey.com

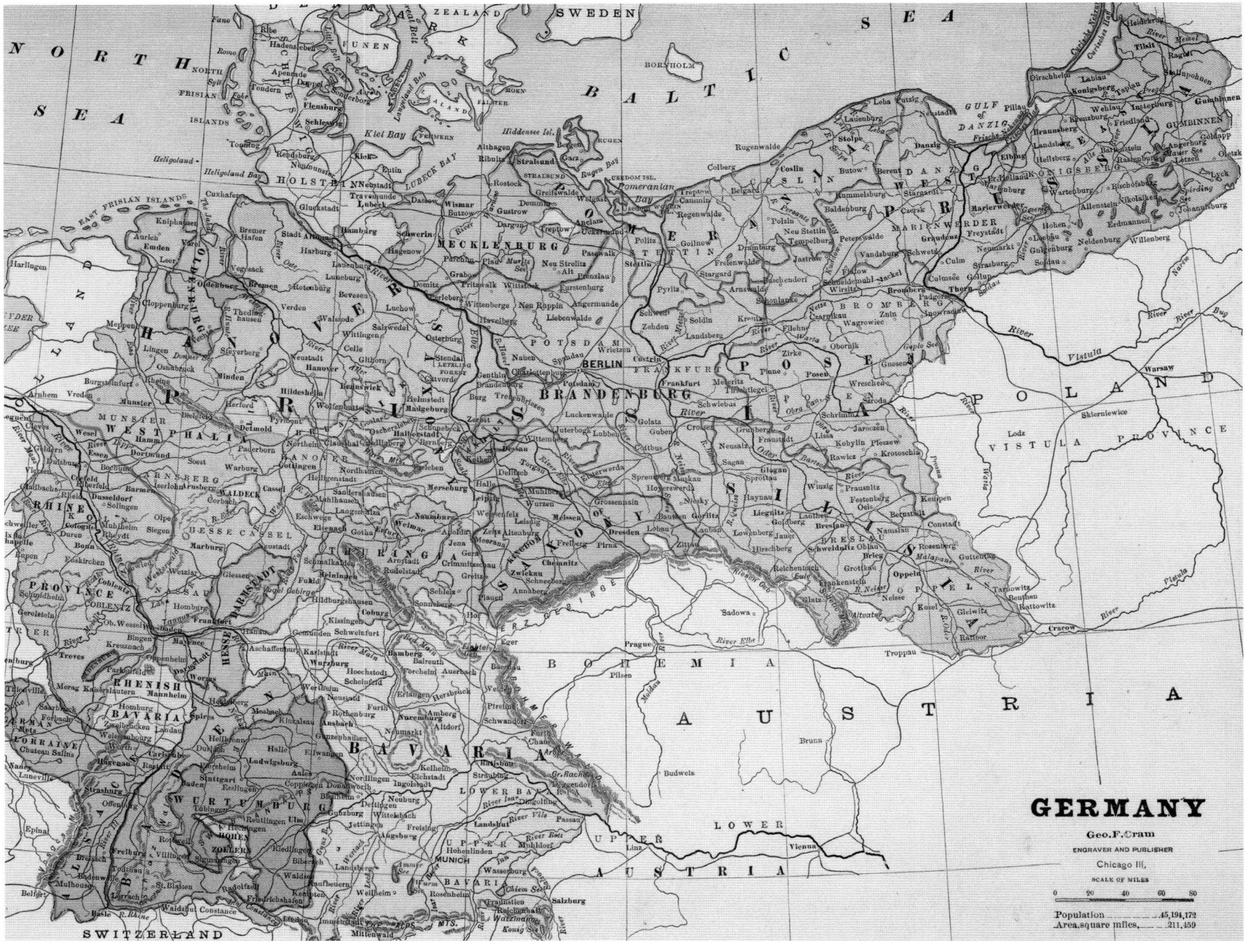
GERMANY
Geo. F. Cram
ENGRAVER AND PUBLISHER
Chicago Ill.
SCALE OF MILES
0 20 40 60 80
Population 45,194,172
Area, square miles 211,459
NORTH SEA
BALTIC SEA
SWEDEN
ZEALAND
FUNEN
BORNHOLM
ALAND
FALSTER
MOEN
RUGEN
USEDOM ISL.
Heligoland
Heligoland Bay
FRISIAN ISLANDS
EAST FRISIAN ISLANDS
Kiel Bay
Hiddensee Isl.
Pomeranian Bay
GULF of DANZIG
Frisches Haff
Kurisches Haff
HOLSTEIN
LUBECK BAY
MECKLENBURG
HANNOVER
PRUSSIA
POMERANIA
BRANDENBURG
BERLIN
POTSDAM
FRANKFURT
POSEN
BROMBERG
WEST PRUSSIA
EAST PRUSSIA
KONIGSBERG
GUMBINNEN
MARIENWERDER
DANZIG
WESTPHALIA
MUNSTER
RHINE PROVINCE
COLOGNE
COBLENZ
HESSE CASSEL
WALDECK
HESSE DARMSTADT
THURINGIA
SAXONY
SILESIA
BRESLAU
OPPELN
POLAND
VISTULA PROVINCE
Warsaw
Lodz
Cracow
Vistula
River Bug
River Elbe
Prague
BOHEMIA
Pilsen
AUSTRIA
Vienna
Brunn
Budweis
Troppau
Sadowa
Tarnowitz
Beuthen
Rattowitz
Gleiwitz
Rathbor
Glatz
Neisse
Breslau
Liegnitz
Lowenberg
Jauer
Hirschberg
Schweidnitz
Brieg
Oppeln
Posen
Bromberg
Thorn
Danzig
Konigsberg
Stettin
Stralsund
Rostock
Lubeck
Hamburg
Bremen
Hanover
Cologne
Frankfurt
Mayence
Munich
Salzburg
Linz
Passau
Ratisbon
Augsburg
Nuremberg
Wurzburg
Cassel
Leipzig
Dresden
Magdeburg
Hamburg
Kiel
Emden
Cuxhaven
Wismar
Schwerin
Hagenow
Parchim
Grabow
Pritzwalk
Wittstock
Perleberg
Wittenberge
Neu Ruppin
Angermunde
Liebenwalde
Havelberg
Stendal
Salzwedel
Celle
Gifhorn
Brunswick
Hildesheim
Hanover
Minden
Osnabruck
Meppen
Leer
Oldenburg
Bremen
Verden
Luneburg
Lauenburg
Harburg
Stade
Bremerhafen
Cloppenburg
Vegesack
Rotenburg
Bevesen
Luchow
Walsode
Wittlingen
Celle
Neustadt
Osterburg
Stendal
Burg
Brandenburg
Genthin
Zerbst
Cothen
Bernburg
Halberstadt
Magdeburg
Helmstedt
Wolfenbuttel
Goslar
Osterode
Northeim
Gottingen
Nordhausen
Eisleben
Halle
Merseburg
Leipzig
Wurzen
Meissen
Grossenhain
Bautzen
Goerlitz
Lobau
Zittau
Pirna
Freiberg
Chemnitz
Zwickau
Annaberg
Schneeberg
Zeitz
Altenburg
Naumburg
Weimar
Jena
Gotha
Erfurt
Eisenach
Mulhausen
Sondershausen
Nordhausen
Eschwege
Cassel
Marburg
Giessen
Wetzlar
Fulda
Hildburghausen
Coburg
Meiningen
Kissingen
Schweinfurt
Gemunden
Aschaffenburg
Karlsruhe
Wurzburg
Bamberg
Bayreuth
Hochstadt
Forchheim
Auerbach
Erlangen
Hersbruck
Amberg
Altdorf
Nuremberg
Ansbach
Rothenburg
Neustadt
Furth
Schwandorf
Pfreimd
Weiden
Eger
Frankfurt
Hanau
Wiesbaden
Mayence
Bingen
Kreuznach
Oppenheim
Worms
Mainz
Darmstadt
Heidelberg
Mannheim
Kaiserslautern
Landau
Spires
Karlsruhe
Rastatt
Baden
Strasburg
Colmar
Mulhouse
Belfort
Epinal
Nancy
Metz
Luneville
Saarbruck
Trier
Treves
Coblentz
Cologne
Duren
Bonn
Dusseldorf
Elberfeld
Barmen
Solingen
Dortmund
Essen
Bochum
Hamm
Paderborn
Detmold
Minden
Osnabruck
Munster
Emden
Leer
Oldenburg
Bremen
Hamburg
Altona
Lubeck
Wismar
Rostock
Stralsund
Greifswald
Stettin
Colberg
Kolberg
Danzig
Konigsberg
Tilsit
Memel
Insterburg
Gumbinnen
Allenstein
Thorn
Bromberg
Posen
Breslau
Liegnitz
Glogau
Frankfurt
Cottbus
Guben
Luckenwalde
Wittenberg
Dessau
Halle
Leipzig
Dresden
Chemnitz
Zwickau
Gera
Jena
Weimar
Erfurt
Gotha
Eisenach
Fulda
Kassel
Marburg
Giessen
Wetzlar
Coblentz
Cologne

Illustration © David Rumsey Map Collection, www.davidrumsey.com

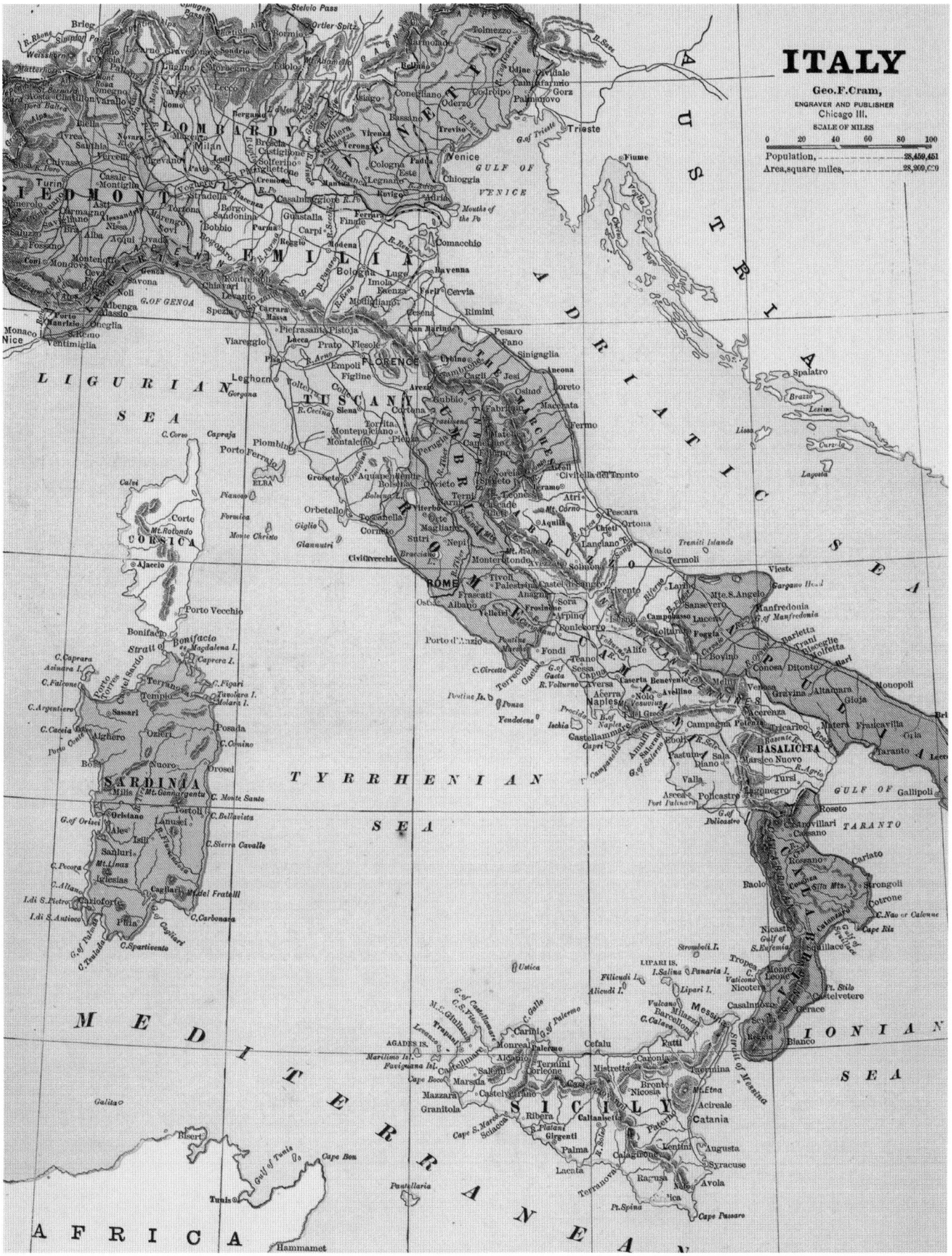
ITALY
Geo.F.Cram,
ENGRAVER AND PUBLISHER
Chicago Ill.
SCALE OF MILES
0 20 40 60 80 100
Population, 28,450,451
Area, square miles, 28,900,000
LIGURIAN SEA
TYRRHENIAN SEA
ADRIATIC SEA
IONIAN SEA
MEDITERRANEAN
AFRICA
AUSTRIA
PIEDMONT
LOMBARDY
VENETIA
EMILIA
TUSCANY
FLORENCE
ROME
CORSICA
SARDINIA
SICILY
BASILICATA
GULF OF VENICE
GULF OF GENOA
GULF OF TARANTO
GULF OF Gallipoli
Venice
Trieste
Fiume
Genoa
Milan
Turin
Naples
Palermo
Messina
Catania
Tunis
Bisert
Hammamet
Cape Bon
Gulf of Tunis
Strait of Messina
Mt. Etna
Mt. Vesuvius
Mt. Rotondo
Mt. Gennargentu
Mt. Linas
Mt. Corno
Mt. Stilo
Mt. Ortler Spitz
Stelvio Pass
Mt. Rosa
Mt. Pecora

Illustration © David Rumsey Map Collection, www.davidrumsey.com

EASTERN HEMISPHERE

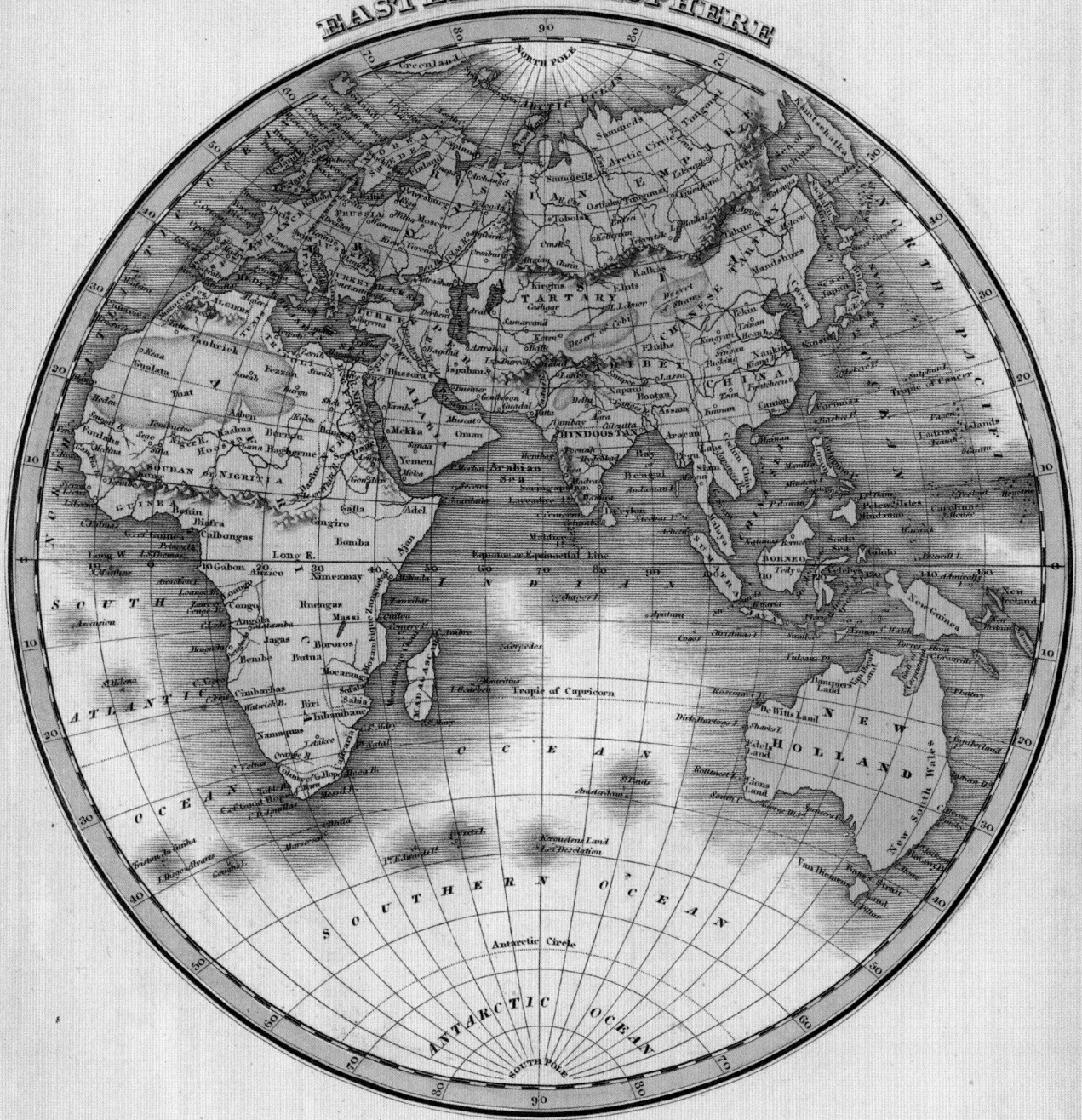

Young & Delleker Sc.

Published by A. Finley Philad.a

Illustration © David Rumsey Map Collection, www.davidrumsey.com

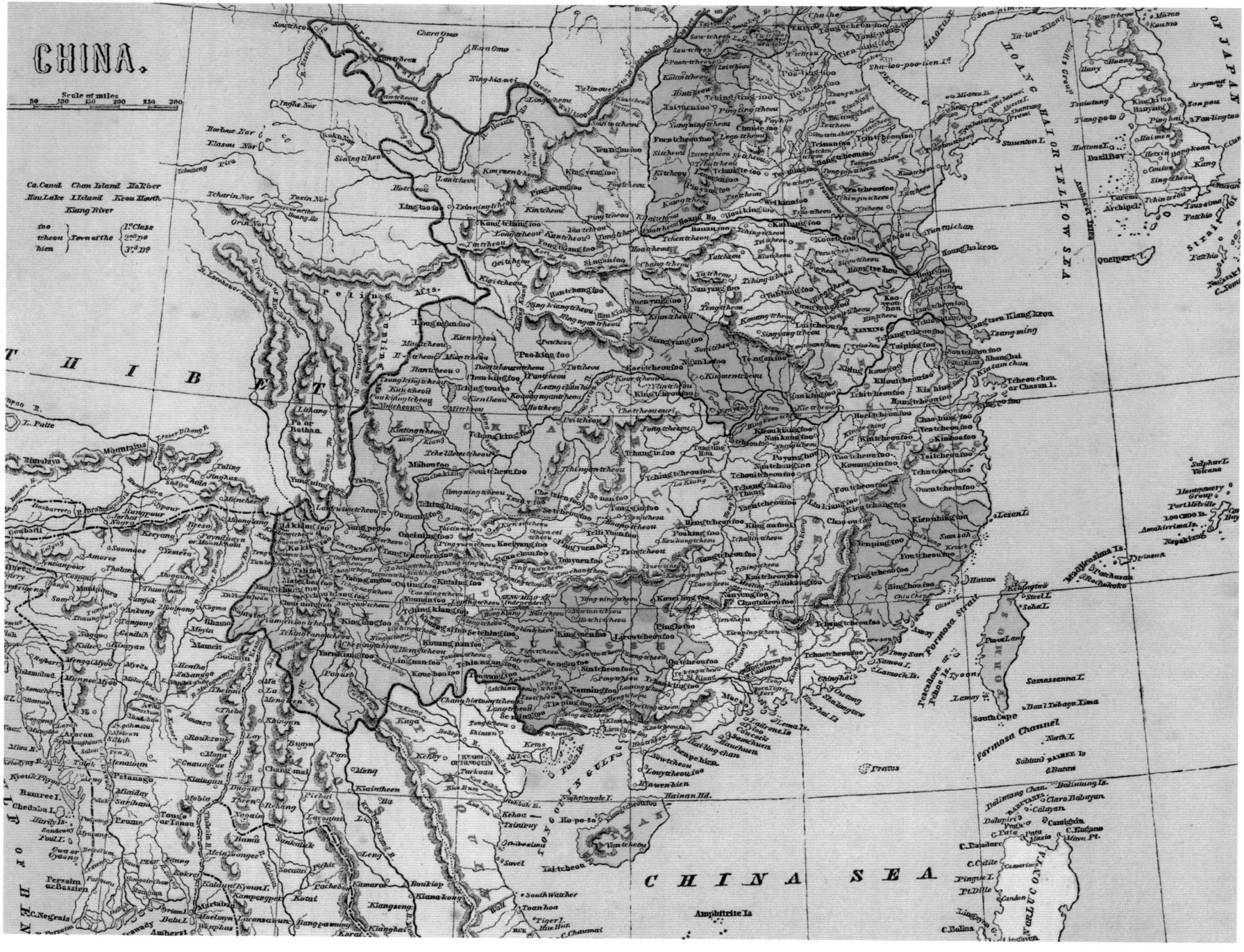
CHINA.
Scale of miles
50 100 150 200 250 300
Ca. Canal
Chan Island
Ho River
Hou Lake
I. Island
Keou Mouth
Kiang River
Fou
tcheou
hien
Town of the
1st Class
2nd Do
3rd Do
Peking
Mts.
TIBET
CHINA SEA
Amphitrite Is
Formosa Strait
Formosa Channel
Pescadores or Pang Hu Is.
Hainan Ild.
Tonkin Gulf
Pratas
Macao
Hong Kong
Canton
Hainan
Hong Kong
Macao
Pratas
Hainan Ild.
Tonkin Gulf
Amphitrite Is
Formosa Strait
Formosa Channel
Pescadores or Pang Hu Is.

Illustration © David Rumsey Map Collection, www.davidrumsey.com

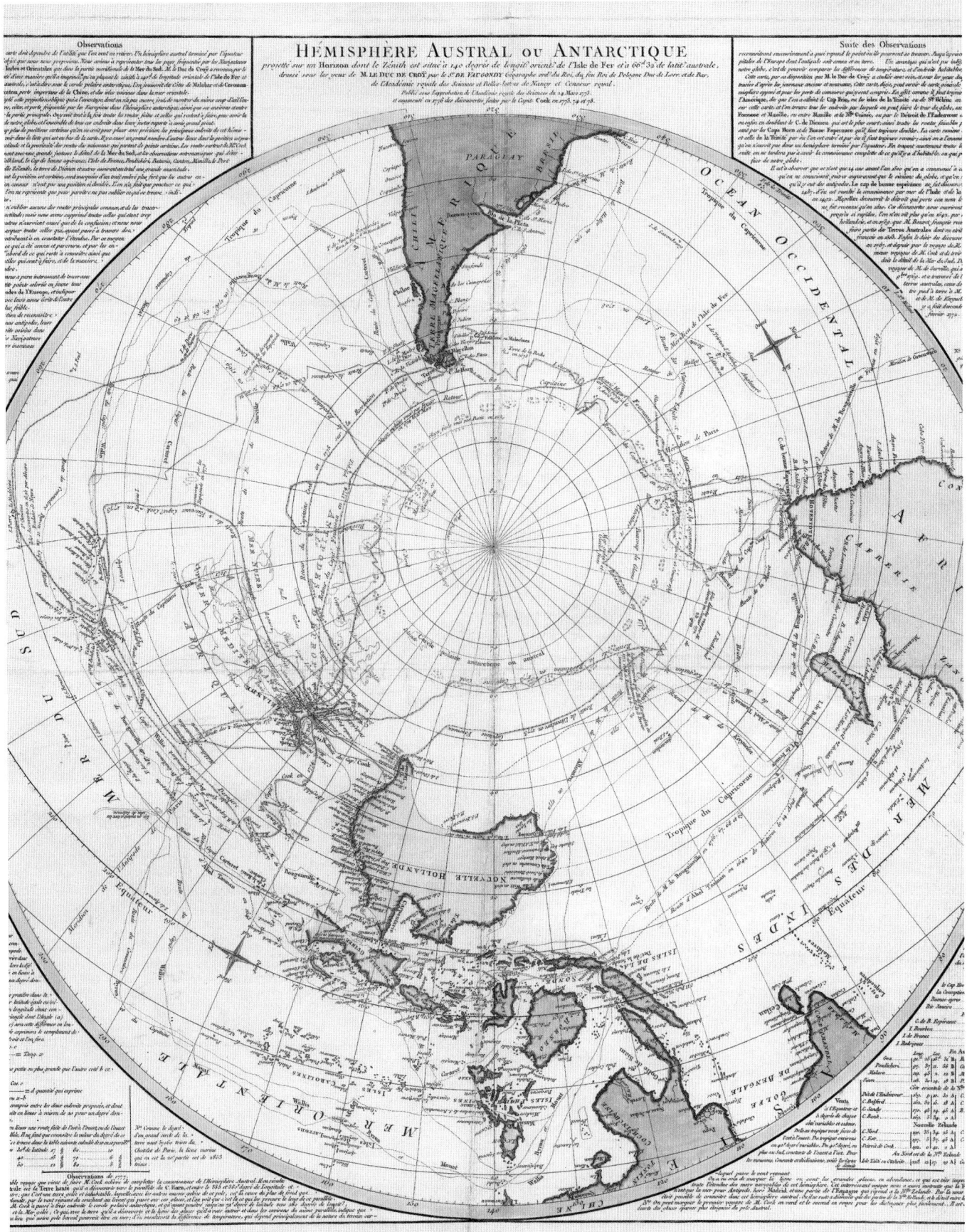
HÉMISPHÈRE AUSTRAL ou ANTARCTIQUE
projetté sur un Horizon dont le Zénith est situé à 140 degrés de longitude orienté de l'Isle de Fer et à 66d 33' de latitude australe, dressé sous les yeux de M. LE DUC DE CROY par le Sr DR VAUGONDY Géographe ordinaire du Roi, du feu Roi de Pologne Duc de Lorr. et de Bar, de l'Académie royale des Sciences et Belles lettres de Nancy et Censeur royal.
Observations
Suite des Observations
OCEAN OCCIDENTAL
Tropique du Capricorne
Equateur
Meridien de Paris
Meridien de l'Isle de Fer
NOUVELLE HOLLANDE
ISLES DE BRESALE
ISLES DE SOLOMON
ISLES DE LA SONDE
ISLES DE CAROLINES
ISLES DE MARIANNES
ISLES DE PHILIPPINES
MER DU SUD
MER ORIENTALE
MER DES INDES
CHINE
TARTARIE
PARAGUAY
BRESIL
CHILI
TERRE MAGELLANIQUE
Observations de 1777.

Illustration © David Rumsey Map Collection, www.davidrumsey.com

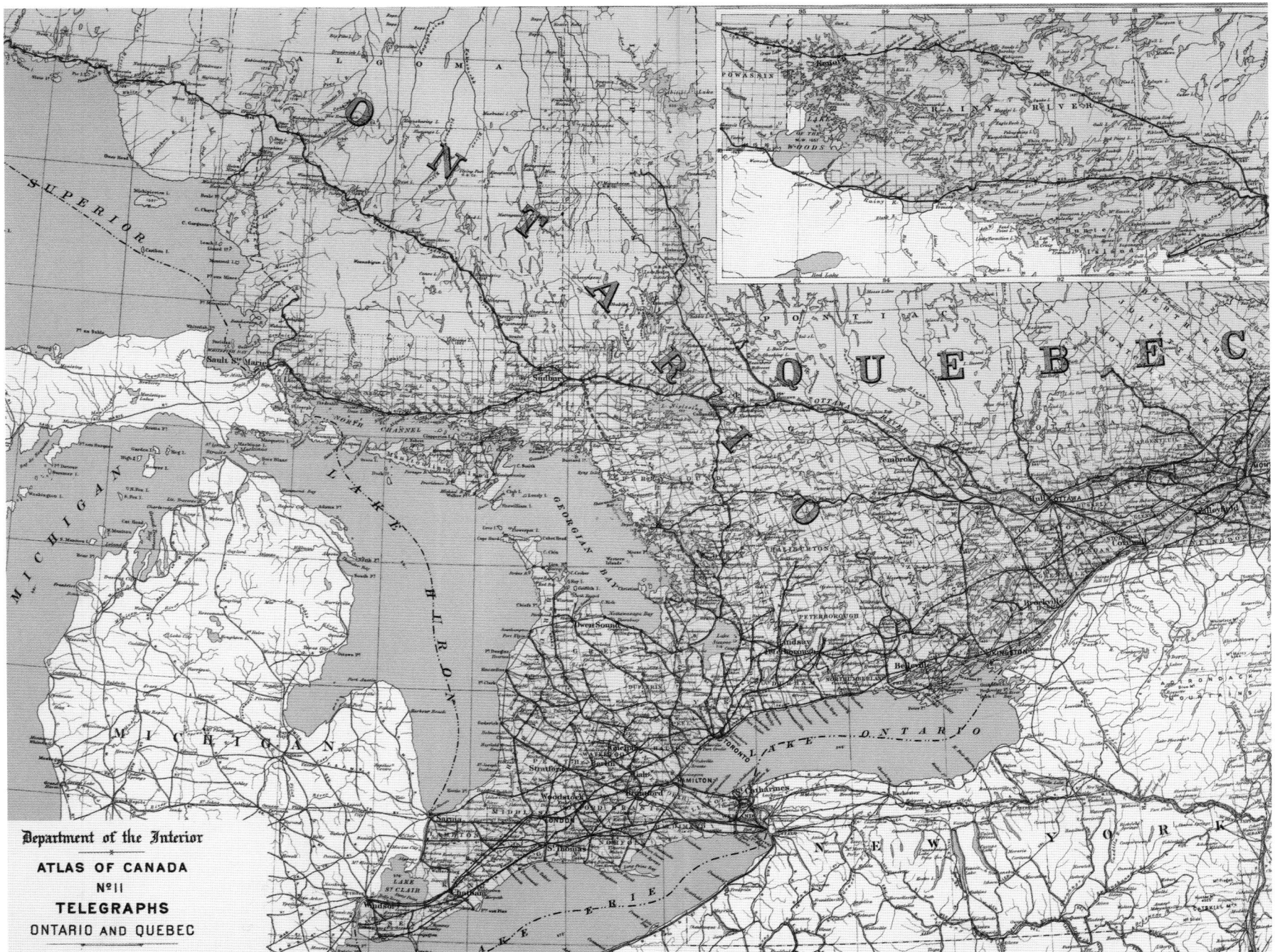
Department of the Interior
ATLAS OF CANADA
Nº 11
TELEGRAPHS
ONTARIO AND QUEBEC
Scale, 1:2,217,600 or 35 Miles to 1 Inch
ONTARIO
QUEBEC
LAKE SUPERIOR
LAKE HURON
LAKE ERIE
LAKE ONTARIO
MICHIGAN
NEW YORK
ALGOMA
Sault St Marie
Sudbury
Pembroke
Owen Sound
Lindsay
Peterborough
Belleville
Brockville
Stratford
Woodstock
London
Sarnia
St Thomas
Chatham
Windsor
Hamilton
St Catharines
Toronto
Ottawa
Rainy River
Rainy Lake
Lake of the Woods
Fowassin
Red Lake
Lake St Clair
Georgian Bay
North Channel
Muskoka
Parry Sound
Nipissing
Pontiac
Ottawa
Lennox
Hastings
Northumberland
Durham
Victoria
Haliburton
Peterborough
Simcoe
Dufferin
Wellington
Grey
Bruce
Huron
Perth
Middlesex
Elgin
Kent
Essex
Lambton
Brant
Norfolk
Haldimand
York
Ontario
Adirondack Mountains
Catskill Mts

Illustration © David Rumsey Map Collection, www.davidrumsey.com

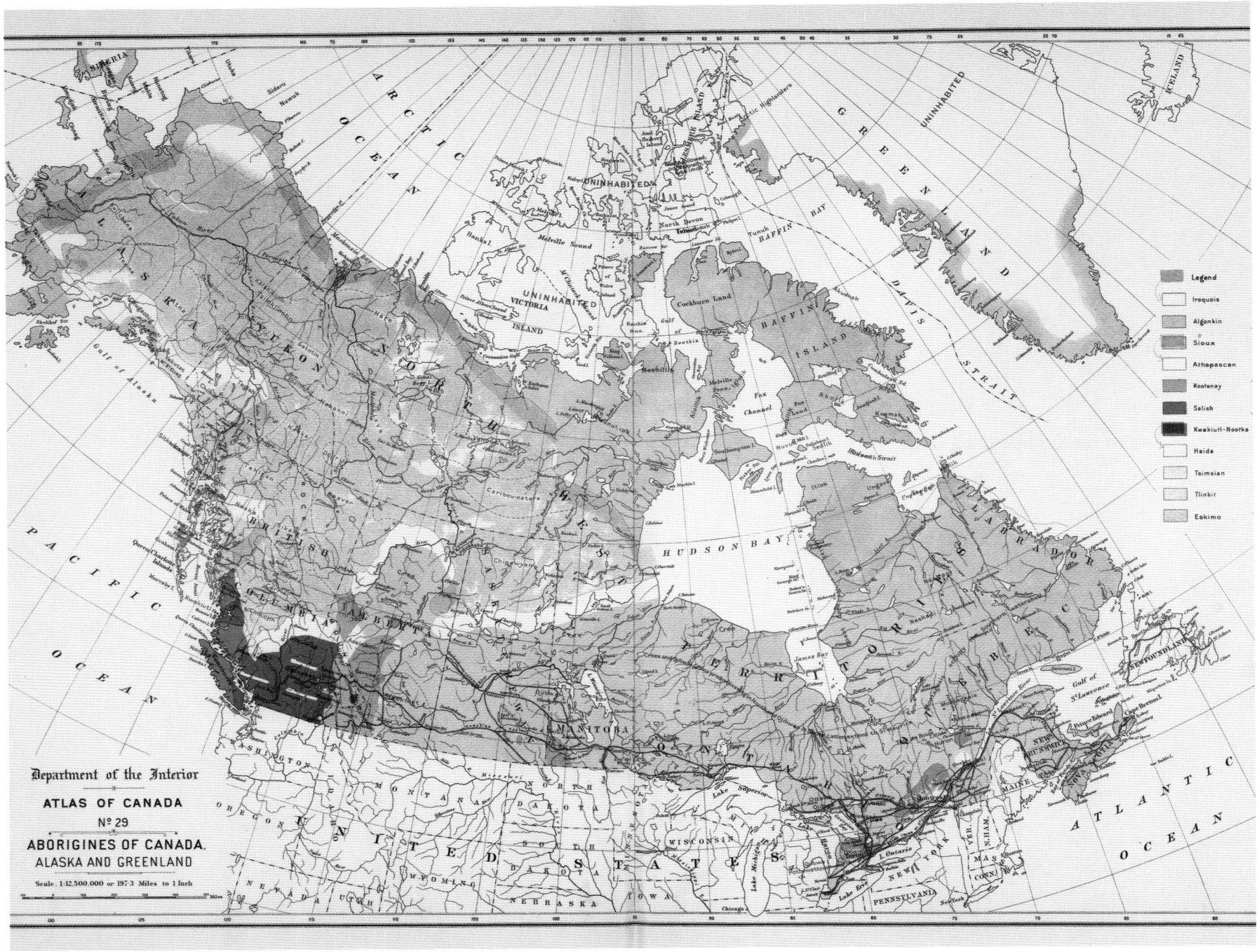
Department of the Interior
ATLAS OF CANADA
Nº 29
ABORIGINES OF CANADA,
ALASKA AND GREENLAND
Scale, 1:12,500,000 or 197·3 Miles to 1 Inch
Legend
Iroquois
Algonkin
Sioux
Athapascan
Kootenay
Salish
Kwakiutl-Noorka
Haida
Tsimsian
Tlinkit
Eskimo
ARCTIC OCEAN
PACIFIC OCEAN
ATLANTIC OCEAN
GREENLAND
UNINHABITED
HUDSON BAY
BAFFIN ISLAND
BAFFIN BAY
DAVIS STRAIT
UNITED STATES
ALASKA
YUKON
NORTH WEST TERRITORIES
BRITISH COLUMBIA
ALBERTA
MANITOBA
ONTARIO
QUEBEC
LABRADOR
NEWFOUNDLAND
NEW BRUNSWICK
NOVA SCOTIA
PRINCE EDWARD I.
CAPE BRETON I.
MAINE
NEW YORK
PENNSYLVANIA
WISCONSIN
MONTANA
NORTH DAKOTA
SOUTH DAKOTA
WYOMING
NEBRASKA
IOWA
NEVADA
UTAH
OREGON
WASHINGTON
Lake Superior
Lake Michigan
Lake Huron
L. Ontario
Lake Erie
Hudson Strait
Gulf of St. Lawrence
St. Lawrence River
Gulf of Alaska
Cockburn Land
Fox Channel
Melville Sound
Victoria Island
Banks I.
Southampton I.
Mackenzie River
Yukon River
Saskatchewan River
Chicago
New York
Quebec
Montreal
Ottawa
Toronto
Winnipeg
Vancouver
Victoria
Dawson
Sitka
Chicago
Boston
Washington
Chicago
ICELAND
SIBERIA

Illustration © David Rumsey Map Collection, www.davidrumsey.com

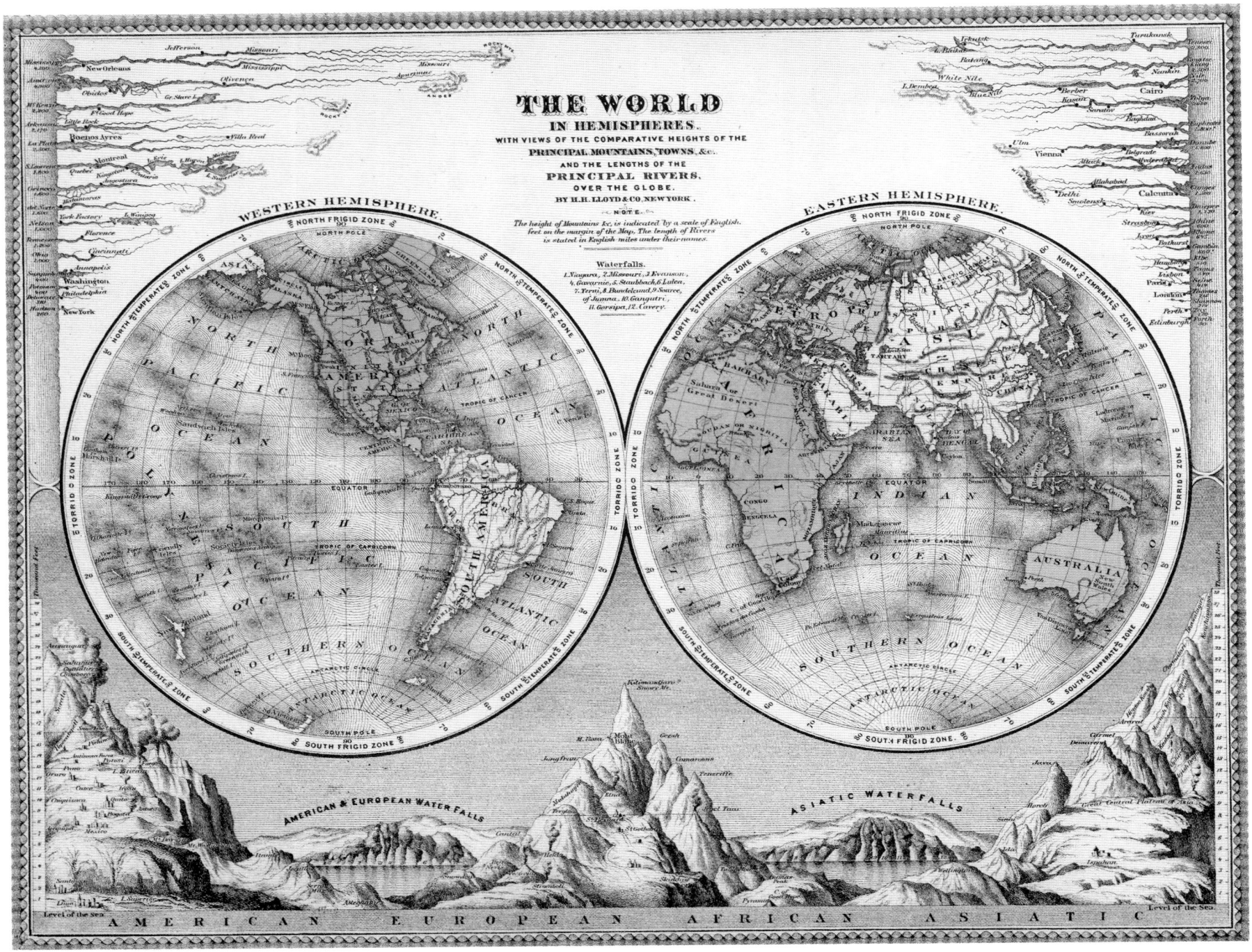
THE WORLD
IN HEMISPHERES.
WITH VIEWS OF THE COMPARATIVE HEIGHTS OF THE
PRINCIPAL MOUNTAINS, TOWNS, &c.
AND THE LENGTHS OF THE
PRINCIPAL RIVERS,
OVER THE GLOBE.
BY H.H. LLOYD & CO. NEW YORK.
NOTE.
The height of Mountains &c, is indicated by a scale of English feet on the margin of the Map. The length of Rivers is stated in English miles under their names.
Waterfalls.
1. Niagara, 2. Missouri, 3. Evenson, 4. Gavarnie, 5. Staubbach, 6. Lulea, 7. Terni, 8. Bundelcund, 9. Source of Jumna, 10. Gangutri, 11. Gersipa, 12. Cavery.
WESTERN HEMISPHERE.
EASTERN HEMISPHERE.
NORTH FRIGID ZONE
NORTH TEMPERATE ZONE
TORRID ZONE
SOUTH TEMPERATE ZONE
SOUTH FRIGID ZONE
NORTH POLE
SOUTH POLE
EQUATOR
TROPIC OF CANCER
TROPIC OF CAPRICORN
ARCTIC CIRCLE
ANTARCTIC CIRCLE
NORTH PACIFIC OCEAN
NORTH ATLANTIC OCEAN
SOUTH PACIFIC OCEAN
SOUTH ATLANTIC OCEAN
SOUTHERN OCEAN
ANTARCTIC OCEAN
INDIAN OCEAN
AUSTRALIA
AMERICAN & EUROPEAN WATER FALLS
ASIATIC WATERFALLS
Level of the Sea
AMERICAN
EUROPEAN
AFRICAN
ASIATIC

Illustration © David Rumsey Map Collection, www.davidrumsey.com

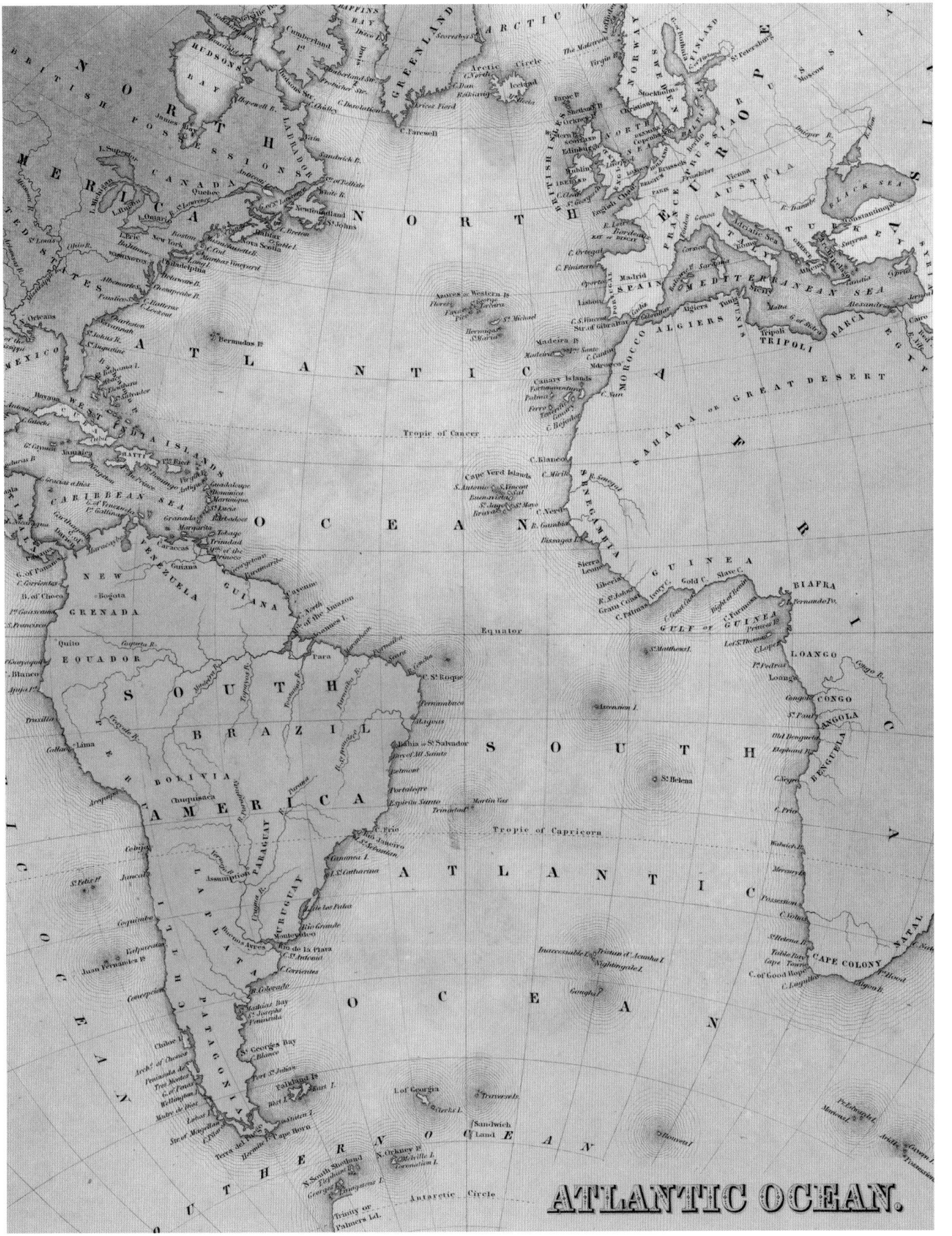
ATLANTIC OCEAN.
NORTH AMERICA
SOUTH AMERICA
NORTH ATLANTIC OCEAN
SOUTH ATLANTIC OCEAN
SOUTHERN OCEAN
EUROPE
AFRICA
ARCTIC OCEAN
GREENLAND
BRITISH POSSESSIONS
CANADA
UNITED STATES
MEXICO
WEST INDIA ISLANDS
CARIBBEAN SEA
NEW GRENADA
VENEZUELA
GUIANA
BRAZIL
BOLIVIA
PARAGUAY
URUGUAY
LA PLATA
PATAGONIA
EQUADOR
PERU
CHILI
NORWAY
SWEDEN
FINLAND
RUSSIA
AUSTRIA
TURKEY
SPAIN
FRANCE
ITALY
MEDITERRANEAN SEA
BLACK SEA
MOROCCO
ALGIERS
TRIPOLI
SAHARA OR GREAT DESERT
SENEGAMBIA
GUINEA
GULF OF GUINEA
BIAFRA
LOANGO
CONGO
ANGOLA
BENGUELA
CAPE COLONY
NATAL
Tropic of Cancer
Tropic of Capricorn
Equator
Antarctic Circle
Bermudas Is
Azores or Western Is
Madeira Is
Canary Islands
Cape Verd Islands
St Helena
Falkland Is
Sandwich Land
Trinidad
Martin Vaz
Tristan d'Acunha I.
Inaccessible I.
Nightingale I.
Gough I.
Bouvet I.
St Paul's I.
Ascension I.
St Matthew I.
Fernando Po
Prince's Is
St Thomas
Lat. St Thomas
Cape Horn
Cape Pillar
Cape Tourle
C. of Good Hope
C. Lagullas
Table Bay
Algoa B.
Port Natal
Sandwich Is
Juan Fernandez Is
Prince Edward I.
Tristan d'Acunha I.
Nightingale I.
Gough I.
Bouvet I.
St Paul's I.
Ascension I.
St Helena

Illustration © Shutterstock.com/steve estvanik

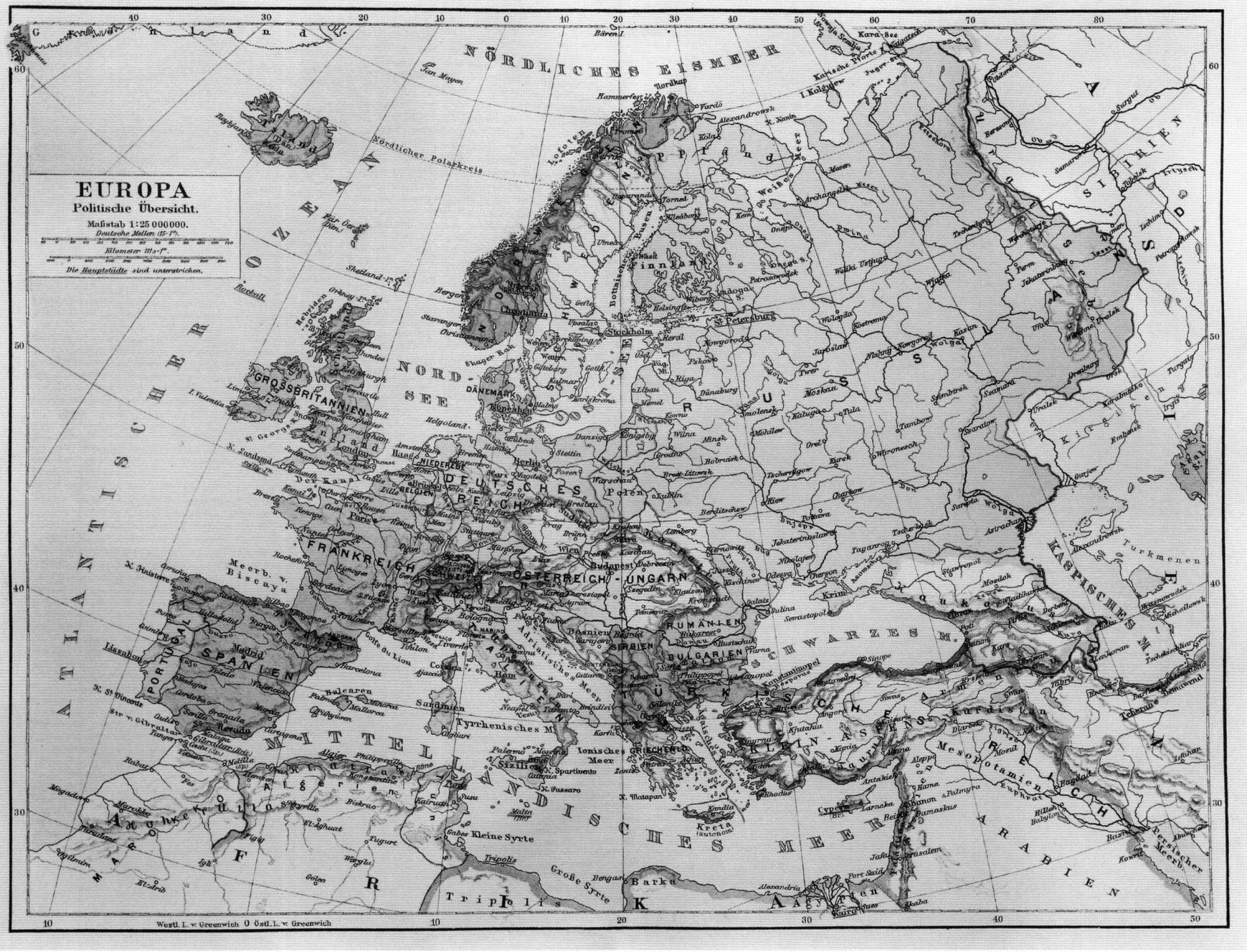
EUROPA
Politische Übersicht.
Maßstab 1:25 000000.
Deutsche Meilen (15 = 1°).
Kilometer (111 = 1°).
Die Hauptstädte sind unterstrichen.
NÖRDLICHES EISMEER
ATLANTISCHER OZEAN
NORD-SEE
OSTSEE
MITTELLÄNDISCHES MEER
SCHWARZES M.
KASPISCHE M.
ARABIEN
SIBIRIEN
GROSSBRITANNIEN
England
London
IRLAND
DÄNEMARK
Kopenhagen
NIEDERLANDE
BELGIEN
DEUTSCHES REICH
Berlin
Hamburg
Leipzig
Dresden
Frankfurt
Wien
Prag
Budapest
Paris
FRANKREICH
Lyon
Marseille
Bordeaux
Toulouse
Nizza
Genua
Mailand
Turin
Venedig
Rom
Neapel
Palermo
Messina
Sizilien
Sardinien
Korsika
Mallorca
Balearen
Madrid
SPANIEN
Barcelona
Valencia
Sevilla
Granada
Malaga
Lissabon
PORTUGAL
Gibraltar
Algier
Algerien
Tunis
Tripolis
Kleine Syrte
Große Syrte
Barka
Ägypten
Kairo
Alexandria
Port Said
Suez
Akaba
Jerusalem
Damaskus
Beirut
Tyrrhenisches M.
Ionisches Meer
GRIECHENLAND
Kreta (autonom)
Rhodus
Smyrna
Konstantinopel
Adriatisches Meer
Bosnien
Serbien
RUMÄNIEN
Bukarest
BULGARIEN
Sofia
TÜRKEI
KLEIN-ASIEN
Kurdistan
Mesopotamien
Bagdad
Persischer Meerb.
Meerb. v. Biscaya
Nordkap
Hammerfest
Tromsö
Christiania
Bergen
Stockholm
Upsala
Helsingfors
St. Petersburg
Moskau
Kiew
Odessa
Sebastopol
Krim
Kaukasus
Tiflis
Baku
Astrachan
Wolga
Ural
Turkmenen
Kirgisen
Nordlicher Polarkreis
Shetland-I.
Orkney-I.
Hebriden
Rockall
Island
Grönland
Jan Mayen
Bären-I.
Kara-See
Weißes Meer
Kola
Archangelsk
Petrozawodsk
Ladoga S.
Onega S.
Wolga
Kostroma
Jaroslawl
Nishnij Nowgorod
Kasan
Samara
Saratow
Tambow
Woronesch
Charkow
Kursk
Orel
Tula
Kaluga
Smolensk
Mohilew
Minsk
Wilna
Kowno
Riga
Dünaburg
Pskow
Tschernigow
Kiew
Berditschew
Lemberg
Krakau
Warschau
Posen
Danzig
Königsberg
Stettin
Lübeck
Hamburg
Bremen
Hannover
Leipzig
Dresden
Breslau
Prag
Wien
Budapest
Szegedin
Temesvar
Kronstadt
Jassy
Kischinew
Odessa
Cherson
Sebastopol
Jekaterinoslaw
Taganrog
Rostow
Astrachan
Tschernigow
Gomel
Bobruisk
Smolensk
Moskau
Jekaterinburg
Perm
Samara
Saratow
Tiraspol
Kischinew
Galatz
Bukarest
Sofia
Philippopel
Konstantinopel
Smyrna
Rhodus
Kreta
Alexandria
Port Said
Suez
Akaba
Jerusalem
Damaskus
Beirut
Aleppo
Mossul
Bagdad
Basra
Persischer Meerb.
Westl. L. v. Greenwich 0 Östl. L. v. Greenwich

Illustration © Shutterstock.com/Nicku

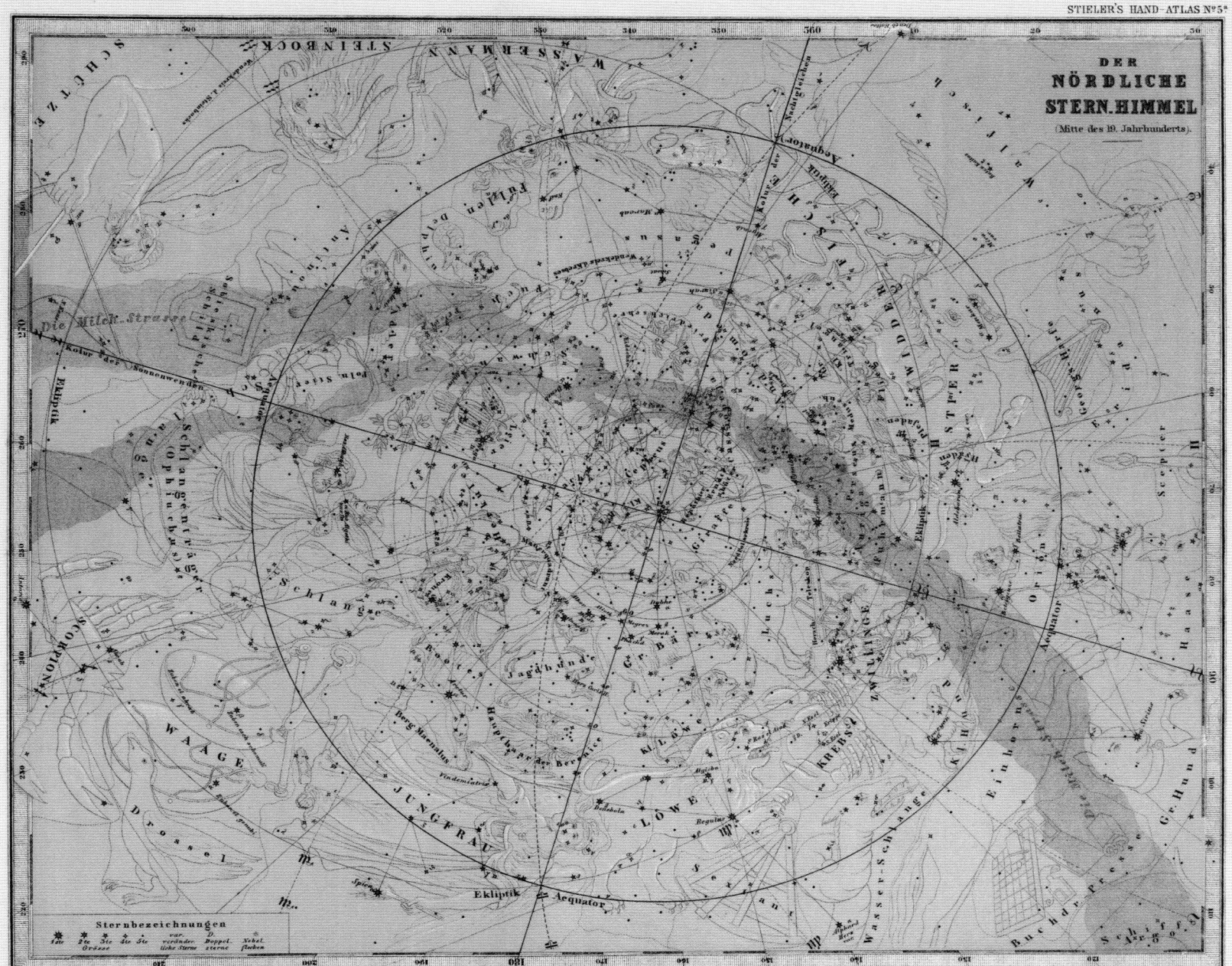

Entw. v. A. Stieler. Neue Aufl. berichtigt v. Dr C. Bruhns.

GOTHA: JUSTUS PERTHES
1874.

Illustration © David Rumsey Map Collection, www.davidrumsey.com

DER NÖRDLICHE STERN-HIMMEL.

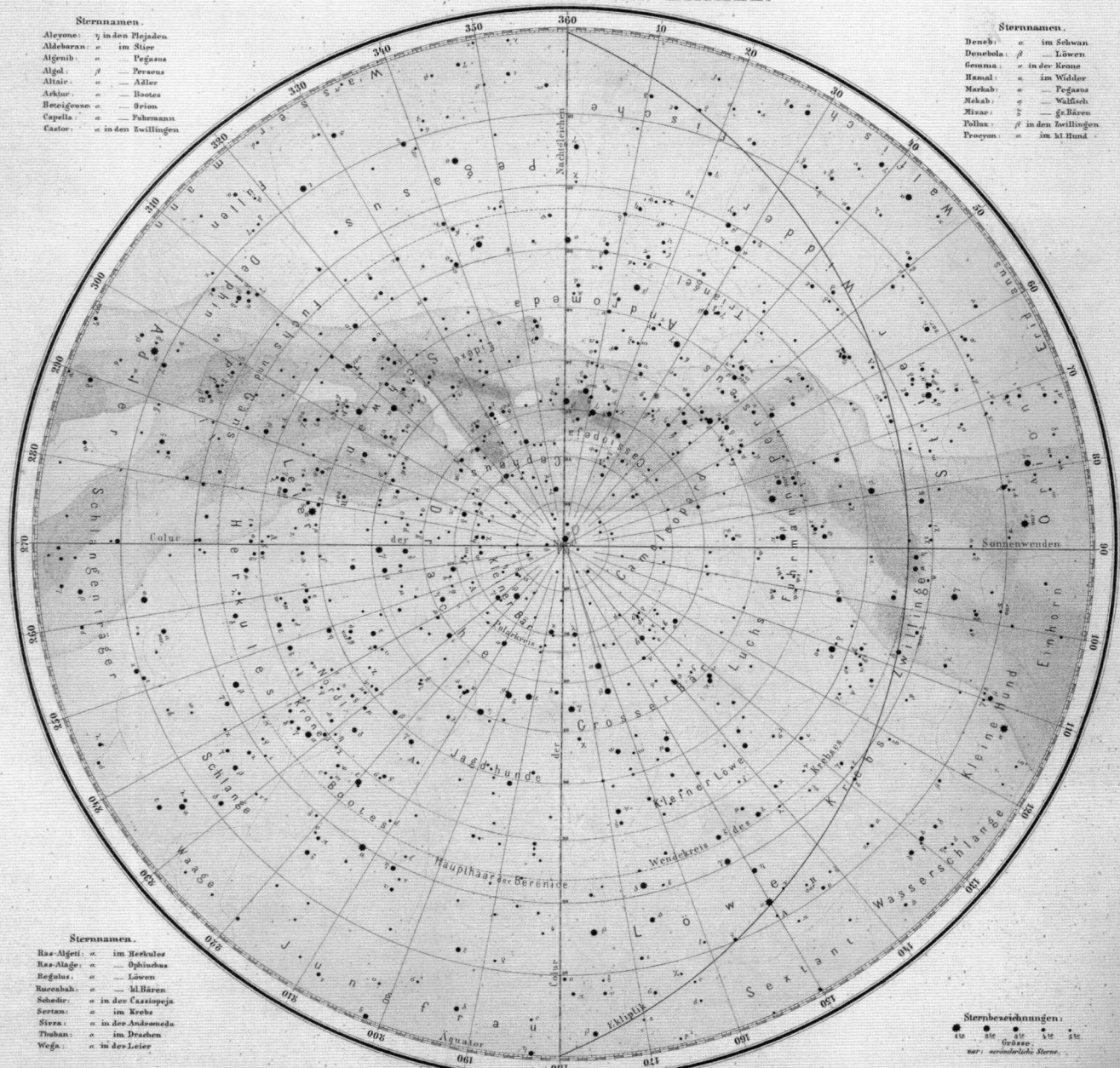

Entw. u. gez. v. Dr. H. J. Klein.

Druck u. Verlag v. C. Flemming in Glogau.

Illustration © David Rumsey Map Collection, www.davidrumsey.com